PRISON

TO

PRAISE

Merlin R. Carothers is well-known throughout the Christian community. His books have sold over 16 million copies. His unique concept of "praise in all things" brings results that can only be termed miraculous.

Merlin R. Carothers may be the only author to have served as a paratrooper in World War II, as a guard for General Dwight D. Eisenhower, and later as a Lt. Colonel in the U.S. Army Chaplaincy in Korea, the Dominican Republic conflict, and in Vietnam.

During these conflicts Merlin Carothers learned amazing things that changed his life. Many people who have read this book have come to enjoy a happiness they never expected to experience. Christians have been overwhelmed to learn that they can live in peace as they discover the secrets of a life of praise.

Read this book and you will understand how to be victorious over the circumstances of your lifc!

"Be joyful always;
pray continually;
give thanks in all
circumstances for
this is God's will
for you"!

I Thessalonians 5:16-18

CONTENTS

Chapters

1

Prisoner

There was the touch of cold metal against my left wrist and the harsh voice in my ear: "This is the FBI. You are under arrest."

I'd been relaxing in the back seat of the car with my left arm hanging out the window. The car was stolen and I was AWOL from the Army.

Being AWOL didn't bother me. It was the getting caught that hurt my pride. I'd always considered myself capable of doing my own thing and getting away with it. Now I had to suffer the humiliation of the jail cell, stand in line for lousy cold chow, go back to the lonely cell and the hard bunk with nothing to do but stare at the wall. How could I have been stupid enough to get into a mess like this?

I'd been a pretty independent fellow from the time I was twelve. That's when my father died suddenly, leaving my mother alone with three boys to raise. My brothers were seven and one, and Mother started taking in washings and went on relief to keep us alive. She always talked about Dad being in heaven and how God would take care of us, but with the intensity of a twelve-year-old I turned in fury against a God who could treat us that way.

I delivered papers after school until long after dark each night, determined to make my way in

1

life. I was going to make the most of it. Somehow I felt I had it coming. I had a right to grab for all I could get.

When Mother remarried, I went to live with some of Dad's old friends. I went to high school, but never quit working. After school and all summer I worked. As a food packer, shipping clerk, linotype operator, and one summer as a lumberjack in Pennsylvania.

I started college, but ran out of money and had to go to work. This time I got a job with B&W Steel as a steel chipper and grinder. Not a very pleasant job, but it kept me in top physical condition. Part of staying ahead in the rat race of the world was being in top shape physically, and I didn't intend to lose out on any count.

I never did want to join the Army. I wanted to go off to sea with the Merchant Marine. I couldn't think of a more glamorous way to get into action in World War II.

To join the Merchant Marine I had to get reclassified 1-A with the draft board that had given me a deferment to go to college. Before I could make it back to the Merchant Marine, the Army inducted me. They told me I could volunteer for the Navy, which I did, but a freak incident kept me out. I failed the eye test simply because I'd been reading the wrong line on the chart by mistake! So there, against all my efforts, I landed in basic training at Ft. McClellan, Alabama.

I was bored to death. The training was a breeze, and looking for excitement, I volunteered for airborne training at Fort Benning, Georgia.

A rebel at heart, my biggest problem always was in getting along with my superiors. Somehow they picked on me in spite of all my efforts to remain in the background. Once, during physical training in a sawdust pit, I spat on the ground without thinking. The Sergeant saw me, and descended like a storm cloud. "Pick that up in your mouth and carry it out of the area!" he screamed.

You've got to be kidding, I thought, but his red, glowering face indicated he was not. So, humiliated and seething with resentment carefully hidden, I picked up the spit - and a mouthful of sawdust - and carried it "out of the area."

The compensation came when we got our first chance to jump from an airplane in flight. This was living! The kind of excitement I was hungering for. Over the roar of the plane engines came the shouted command: "Get ready. . .stand up. . .hook up. . .stand in the door. . .GO!"

The blast of air makes you feel like a leaf in a gale - and then, as the rope attached to your parachute reaches its end, a bone-jarring jolt. You feel like you've been hit by a ten-ton truck.

Then, as your brain clears, you're in a beautiful silent world; billowing above is the parachute - a giant white arc of silk.

I was a paratrooper, and earned the honor of wearing the glistening jump boots.

Still, I wanted more excitement and volunteered for advanced training as a Demolition Expert. I wanted in on the war effort, and the hotter the action the better, I thought.

After demolition school I returned to Fort Benning to wait for orders to go overseas. I pulled guard at the stockade, had KP, and waited some more. Patience was not my strong point. At the rate the Army was moving, I figured I might miss out on the fun altogether, scrubbing pots and pans till the war ended.

I wasn't going to sit around doing nothing, and with a friend, I decided to go over the hill.

We simply walked out of the camp one day, stole a car, and headed for anyplace. Just in case someone was looking for us, we dropped the first car and stole another and finally ended up in Pittsburgh, Pennsylvania. There we ran out of spending money and decided to pull a stickup.

I had the gun and my friend waited in the car. We'd picked a store that looked like an easy job. My plan was to pull the telephone wiring so they couldn't call the police. Inside the store, I yanked on the telephone wire as hard as I could, but it wouldn't budge. I was frustrated. The gun was in my pocket, the cash register was full of money, but the line to the police was still there. I wasn't about to invite disaster.

So I went back to the car to tell my buddy, and we were just sitting there in the back seat, eating green apples and talking, when the long arm of the law finally caught up with us. We didn't know it, but a six-state alarm had gone out for us, and the FBI was hot on our heels.

Our search for adventure had ended in a pretty sad flop. I was back in the stockade at Fort

Benning where I'd been a guard only a few months earlier. I was sentenced to six months' confinement and immediately started a campaign to get overseas. My fellow prisoners laughed and said, "You wouldn't have gone AWOL if you wanted to go overseas."

I kept insisting I'd gone AWOL because I got bored waiting to be sent overseas.

At last my pleas were heard. I was placed on overseas shipment and went "under guard" to Camp Kilmer, N.J., where I was placed in the stockade to wait for our ship to Europe.

At last, I was on my way. Almost, anyway. The night before our ship was due to sail I was called to the Commander's office where I learned that I wouldn't be sailing with the rest of the men.

"The FBI wants you held and returned to Pittsburgh, Pennsylvania."

Once more I felt the cold steel of handcuffs, and under armed guard I returned to Pittsburgh where a stern judge read the charges and asked: "Guilty or not guilty; how do you plead?"

My mother was there and her tear-filled eyes made me cringe. Not that I was sorry for what I'd done. I wanted out of there and on with some fast living, the sooner the better.

"Guilty, Sir." I had been caught red-handed and somehow I determined it would be the last time. I would learn the tricks and play it safe from now on.

The district attorney carefully explained my past life to the judge who asked the investigating officers for their recommendation.

"Your honor, we recommend leniency."

"What do you want, soldier?" the judge asked me.

"I want to go back in the Army and get into the war," was all I could say.

"I sentence you to five years in the Federal Penitentiary."

His words hit me like a load of bricks from the skies. I was nineteen and would be twenty-four when I got out. I saw my whole life go down the drain.

"Your sentence is temporarily suspended and you will be returned to the Army."

Saved, thank heaven! In less than an hour I was released. But first the district attorney gave me a stern lecture and explained that if I left the Army in less than five years I should report back to his office.

Free at last! I headed back to Fort Dix, New Jersey, only to get another load of bricks on my head. At Fort Dix they looked at my papers and sent me back to the stockade to serve out my six months' sentence for AWOL!

At this point I had only one thought in my head. I wanted to get into the war or bust. Again I started my campaign to get on an overseas shipment. I pestered the command until finally, when four months of my time was completed, I was released. Soon I was on my way across the Atlantic aboard the *Mauretania*.

We were piled six high in the hold, and I was lucky enough to get the top berth. That way I missed the shower of vomit those on the lower berths often received.

Not that I really would have cared. I was thrilled to be on my way, and didn't waste any time. I was out to get as much excitement and as much profit as possible out of the war effort. I had developed one talent during my confinement that now came in handy. I had become quite adept at gambling, and the days and nights of our crossing were spent in this worthwhile endeavor. I accumulated a nice little pile of money, and the only thing that reminded me of the circumstances of our voyage was a brief encounter with a German sub that tried to hit us and missed.

In England we were put on trains that took us to the English Channel. There we boarded small boats and moved out into the choppy waters of the channel. It rained cats and dogs, and on the French side we had to jump into waist-high water and wade ashore.

On the beach we stood dripping wet in line waiting for cold C-rations. Then we rushed again for a train headed east. Without stopping, we crossed France and were transferred to trucks taking us into Belgium. We got there just in time for the Battle of the Bulge with the 82nd Airborne Division.

On my first day in combat, the Commanding Officer saw my record as a Demolition Expert and put me to work making small bombs out of a pile of plastic explosives. The pile was about three feet high, and I pulled up a log and went to work. Another soldier joined me, and I learned that he had been with the unit for many months. While he was telling me about his experiences with the 82nd Airborne, I looked across a field at incoming artillery exploding. The explosions came closer and closer to our position. Out of the corner of my eye I kept watching the other soldier, wondering when he'd give the signal to dive for cover. He had all the experience, and I was just a green replacement; I wasn't going to chicken out.

The explosions came nearer, and my fear mounted. If one of those rounds landed near us . . .the pile of bombs would make one giant crater.

The other fellow sat there paying no attention to the artillery. I wanted desperately to dive for cover, but I wasn't about to show myself a coward. At last the explosions were on the other side of us. They had missed!

Two days later I discovered why the other soldier had played it so cool. The two of us were walking through a forest known to be heavily mined. I carefully examined the trail for any signs of booby traps, but the other fellow was paying no attention to where he was walking. I finally said: "Why aren't you watching for mines?"

"I hope I step on one," he said. "I'm sick and tired of this rotten mess. I want to die."

From that day I kept as much distance as possible between the two of us!

Combat with the 82nd Airborne provided ample excitement. But some of the ugly experiences made further harsh impressions in my angry mind.

At the close of the war I went with the 508th Airborne Regiment to Frankfurt, Germany, where I was selected to serve as guard for General of the Army, Dwight D. Eisenhower. This was a proud moment in my life. I, Merlin Carothers, a personal guard for a Five-star General! I felt I had finally become "big man on campus."

I would have liked to see more action, but the spoils of war weren't so bad either. We lived in plush apartment buildings that had belonged to top German officials. The previous occupants must have had no more than five minutes' notice before they departed. We found family picture albums, weapons and even jewels. My off-duty time was spent in searching for "treasure."

My on-duty time was always fun. One evening I was assigned duty at a gate leading into General Eisenhower's Headquarters Compound. Something special was up. The Duty Officer said, "Pfc. Carothers, this could be a big night. I'll fill you in later."

Some time later the Duty Officer came back and said, "Here it is, Carothers. The W.A.C. Commanding Officer is having a dance for her girls next week, but she didn't invite the paratroopers. When our C.O. called and asked her why, she said she didn't want any "overpaid killers" at their dance.

"The rules say that all assigned female personnel must be inside this gate not later than 9:00 p.m. After 9:00 p.m. no W.A.C. (Women's Army Corps) will pass through this gate until I personally escort them. Take no flak from any-one. I've put you here because I know you won't!"

A few minutes after 9:00 p.m. a jeep, driven by an Army Sergeant, pulled up to the gate. A W.A.C. enlisted girl was seated beside the soldier. I said, "The W.A.C. must get out and stand here by the gate."

"She what?" The Sergeant's anger exploded!

"You heard me."

"Why?"

"No reason. Miss, get out of the jeep now and stand beside me."

Never had I spoken to a Sergeant this way. If he had been an airborne trooper I probably wouldn't have dared.

The Sergeant unloaded a few dozen curse words, but then turned around and left. He knew that as a guard assigned to a gate I had total authority.

From 9:00 until 9:45, twenty W.A.C.s arrived. On previous nights they had come in whenever they desired, but tonight was different. I was in the middle of the hurricane. They were mad - very mad. Such language I heard!

At 10:45 a staff car, driven by a Colonel, pulled up. Never in my career had I even spoken to a full Colonel. I politely gave him my message. "The W.A.C. officer that is with you must join these other ladies who are standing by me."

"Out of the way, Soldier! She is not going to leave this vehicle."

"Yes, Sir, she must."

10

"Soldier, I give you a Direct Order. Move out of the way. We are going through."

A Direct Order is the strongest language an officer can use on a soldier. But he was trying to bluff the wrong private.

In true cowboy fashion I slapped the "45 automatic" from my holster, pulled back the hammer and said, "Miss, step down and join the others. Colonel, turn this vehicle around *now* and leave!"

He did.

At 11:00 p.m. the Duty Officer arrived in a jeep. He told the W.A.C. with the lowest rank to get into his jeep and then said, "Ladies, I'll be back to pick all of you up - one at a time."

The next day the W.A.C. Commander called our C.O. and invited all the airborne troopers to attend her dance.

I was still looking for excitement, and once I almost got more than I bargained for. We were loaded on airplanes for a parachute jump. It was to be a routine training exercise, but we were told that Marlene Dietrich, the movie actress, would be on the ground watching the jump. We were all hoping to land near her.

As soon as I left the plane I began to scan the ground below to see if I could locate the "lady with the beautiful legs." Suddenly I was aware that something was horribly wrong. Around me in the air were terrible screams, and the roar of an airplane engine seemed suddenly to burst right on top of me.

Several hundred troopers were in the air and an airplane had lost engine power and was diving right through us! Parachutes were cut off, and men were plunging to the ground. They were falling all around the spot where Miss Dietrich was standing. My parachute was intact, and when I reached the ground there were dead men all around, and the plane was exploding in flames.

In Frankfurt I had plenty of free time. My idea of a good time usually involved a considerable amount of drinking. It happened that I drank myself into a state of oblivion and other soldiers told me what pranks I had pulled in town the night before. Once I had stretched myself flat on the floor of a German streetcar and dared anyone to walk over me. The other soldiers had roared with laughter and found the whole incident uproariously funny. It never occurred to me that my behavior probably didn't help the image of the American Occupation Army.

I discovered that black marketeering was a quicker and more reliable source of income than gambling. I bought cigarettes from other soldiers for ten dollars a carton. With a suitcase full, I went to the black-market area in town where I could sell the cartons for one hundred dollars apiece. The black-market area was a frequent site of robberies, beatings, and murder, but I didn't care. I kept one hand on a loaded, cocked "45" in my pocket.

Soon I had a suitcase full of ten dollar bills in military money known as scrip. The only problem was to find a way to get the money back to the United States. Tight control limited each soldier to sending home only the amount he was paid by the Army. I stayed awake nights trying to figure a way to beat the system.

At the post office I watched the men line up to convert their monthly pay into money orders. Each man had to have his finance card which listed the exact amount he had been paid. I observed one man with a pile of finance cards, a bag of money, and an armed guard. He was company clerk and was getting money orders for his entire company. I suddenly realized that all I needed was a pile of finance cards!

I located the unit finance clerk and soon learned that he would be willing to provide me with the finance cards for five dollars apiece. I was in business.

I set myself up as the company clerk of my own private company. With the money and the finance cards I went to the post office and had the money orders made out without a hitch!

With this setup I now found new ways to accumulate the military scrip money. I learned that men coming from Berlin would give $1,000 in scrip for a $100 money order. I gladly obliged and then converted the $900 into my own money order. I was on my way to becoming very rich!

The Army announced the decision to send some men to universities throughout Europe. I took the examinations, was selected, and sent to

Bristol University in England. The courses I took were far less important than the fact that we were surrounded by girls who spoke English.

But I did make some steps toward what I believed was my future. I took a course in English Law and another in Business Law. I wanted to know how "the system" worked so I could beat it.

When the university course ended I was transferred back to Germany. There awaited exciting news. My time to return to the U.S. had arrived! I packed my suitcase full of $100 money orders and headed for the glorious shores of home.

At Fort Dix, N.J., they tried to get all of us to sign up for the Army Reserves. The Sergeant giving the pitch said, "Everyone who wants to sign up for the Reserves step up here, sign, and I'll give you your discharge. If you don't sign up now you will have to stay and hear a one-hour lecture on why you *should* sign up."

One hour longer in the Army? No way, I thought. I stepped forward and signed their paper. That split-second decision affected the rest of my life.

I received the long-coveted paper stating I was now a civilian. Free! I had no desire to ever see the inside of an Army post again. I had plenty of money, and life ahead looked rosy.

There was a problem of converting my suitcase full of money orders into crisp, green bills. I couldn't very well walk into the post office in my hometown, Ellwood City, Pennsylvania, and dump the whole stack on the counter. Finally I thought of a solution. One by one I began to send the money orders to a post office in New York. Soon the money began filtering back.

My experiences with the law so far had taught me that I had better get into a profession where I would be able to operate safely within every available loophole. I had always wanted to become a lawyer, so I began the necessary steps to enroll in law school in Pittsburgh, Pennsylvania.

2

Set Free

Grandmother was a sweet old lady, and I thought a great deal of Grandfather, but going to visit them was still an ordeal I avoided whenever possible. They made me nervous. Grandmother always found an opportunity to talk about God.

"I'm doing fine," I'd say. "Don't worry about me."

But she would insist: "You need to give your life to Christ, Merlin."

It bugged me more than I wanted to admit. I hated to hurt Grandmother's feelings, but I didn't have time for any of that religious stuff. I'd just begun to live!

One Sunday evening shortly after I'd come back from Germany, I went to see Grandmother and Grandfather. I quickly realized I'd made a mistake. They were getting ready to go to church.

"Come go with us, Merlin," Grandmother said. "We haven't seen you for so long; we'd love to have you come."

I squirmed in my chair. How could I tactfully get out of this one?

"I'd like to," I said finally. "But some friends have already asked if they could come pick me up."

Grandmother looked disappointed, and as soon as I could get to the phone I began calling everyone I knew. To my dismay I couldn't find anyone who was free to come pick me up.

It was getting close to church time, and I couldn't say to my grandparents: "I just don't want to go."

At the zero hour I had no choice. Off we went together.

The church service was held in a barn, but everyone there seemed to be happy. *Poor people*, I thought, *they don't know anything about real life out there in the world, or they wouldn't waste an evening in a barn*.

The singing began and I picked up a hymn book to follow the words. At least I had to look as if I was with it.

Suddenly I heard a deep voice speak directly in my ear.

"What-what did you say?" I whirled around to find no one behind me.

There was the voice again: "Tonight you must make a decision for Me. If you don't, it will be too late."

I shook my head and said automatically: "Why?"

"It just will be!"

Was I losing my marbles? But the voice was real. It was God, and He knew me! In a flash I suddenly saw it. Why hadn't I seen it before? God was real; He was the answer. In Him was everything I had ever searched for.

"Yes, God," I heard myself mutter. "I'll do it; whatever You want."

The service went on, but I was in another world. This was crazy, but I knew God!

Grandfather was deep in thought beside me. I didn't know it then, but he told me about it later. He was carrying on his own battle with God. For years he'd been smoking and chewing tobacco. Forty years of addiction to the weed had him hooked. Many a time he'd tried to quit, but had been seized with violent headaches and soon was back to chewing and smoking heavier than before.

Now he was sitting next to me in the meeting making his own commitment. "God, if you'll change Merlin, I'll give up my chewing and smoking even if it kills me."

No wonder Grandfather nearly collapsed when I went forward at the end of the meeting to make public the decision I'd made during the singing!

Years later I was at his bedside when his time came to die. He looked up at me and smiled. "Merlin," he said, "I kept my promise to God."

That Sunday night I couldn't wait to get home and read the Bible. I wanted to know God, and I read hungrily page after page. I had a wonderful feeling of excitement inside. It was even better than jumping off an airplane with a parachute. That night God had reached down inside me, and I was changed into a new being. I felt as if I was standing on the threshold of exciting adventures the likes of which I couldn't even begin to imagine. The God of Abraham, Isaac, and Jacob was still alive; the God who parted the Red Sea and spoke through a burning bush and sent His Son to die on a cross - He was my Father too!

I could suddenly understand what my earthly father had tried to tell me. When he was thirty-six years old he was confined to a bed for the first time in his life. Three days later his heart stopped. The doctor was there with an injection, and my father's heart began beating again. He opened his eyes and said: "That won't be necessary, Doctor. I am going to leave now." He raised himself up in bed and looked around the room with a radiant glow on his face.

"Look!" he said. "They are here to take me!" With that he lay back and was gone.

My father had known Jesus Christ as his personal friend and Savior. He had been ready to go.

Now I felt ready too, but even as I voiced the thought to myself, I became aware of an uneasiness, a gnawing at the back of my mind. What was wrong? Show me, God!

Gradually the thought became clearer. The money! All that money. It wasn't mine; I had to give it back!

The decision made, I breathed a sigh of relief. I couldn't wait to get rid of that money. It was like a sickness inside me, and I knew that feeling would be there until the money was gone.

I told the post office, but they said it wasn't any concern of theirs because I hadn't stolen the money orders. I could do with them as I liked.

I still had a whole bunch that I hadn't cashed in yet, so I took the suitcase into the bathroom and began to flush piles of one hundred dollar money orders down the toilet. With each flush I felt a mounting flood of joy inside.

That still left me with the money I had already cashed. I wrote the U.S. Treasury Department and told them how I had acquired the money. They wrote back asking if I had any evidence of how I had gotten the money and the money orders. It was too late; the evidence was flushed down the drain! I told them I had no proof, just the money, and they advised me that all they could do was to accept the money into the Conscience Fund.

Once again I was a poor man, but I would gladly have given away everything I owned for that new life and joy I felt within.

There was one more shadow of the past to be encountered. I returned to Pittsburgh and reported to the district attorney. There were three years remaining on my sentence, and I would now have to be on a parole status for these years. This meant regular reporting and supervision by a parole officer.

The district attorney received me and asked a clerk to get my records. He glanced at them and looked surprised.

"Do you know what you have received?" I knew I'd received Christ, but that could hardly have gotten into my record already.

"No, sir."

"You have received a presidential pardon, signed by President Truman!"

"A pardon?"

"That means your record is completely clear. Just as if you had never gotten involved with the law."

20

I wanted to shout for joy. "Why did I get it?"

The district attorney smiled. "It has something to do with your excellent combat record."

He explained that I was free to go and do anything I wanted to; my case was closed.

"If you ever apply for a federal job you are completely eligible."

"Thank you, Lord." I was overwhelmed. Not only were my sins washed away and the case closed at Calvary, but God had given me a clean start in the eyes of the United States government as well. Not that I ever thought I'd be looking for a job with them again!

But what was I going to do? My motives for becoming a lawyer had been questionable. It seemed clear that God did not want me in that profession. Soon the thought became very persistent. I was to become a minister! Me, in the pulpit? The thought seemed preposterous. "You know me, Lord," I argued. "I like excitement, adventure, even danger. I wouldn't make a very good preacher."

It seemed that God had His plans for me all set. I couldn't sleep nights, and the longer I thought and prayed, the more exciting the whole idea became. If God could make a preacher out of an ex-jailbird, paratrooper, gambler, and black-marketeer, that would be a greater adventure into the unknown than anything I'd ever tried before.

I enrolled in Marion College, a church-related school in Marion, Indiana, and I must have been the most excited student on campus.

To supplement my income from the GI bill, I worked six hours a day in a foundry. I wanted to get through school as fast as possible so I got special permission to take twenty-one hours rather than the maximum seventeen hours allowed per semester.

I worked from 2:00 p.m. until 8:00 p.m., studied until 12:00 p.m., slept until 4:00 a.m., and then studied until 8:00 a.m. when it was time to go to school.

One Sunday I got my first chance to preach in the local jail. I held onto the bars and begged the men to give their lives to Christ. Every week prisoners knelt, holding on to the bars from the other side, and wept their way to faith in Christ.

I went back to school floating on a cloud.

Saturday nights were free, and I got a group of students together to hold outdoor services on the courthouse steps in the center of Marion. To our delight, people came forward to accept Christ. After the service we walked up and down the streets, urging anyone who would listen to let Jesus come into their lives.

I had never been so busy, yet I felt as if I couldn't work hard enough for Jesus Christ. He had saved my life; the least I could do was give Him my time.

I finished the four-year course in two-and-a-half years and enrolled at Asbury Seminary in Wilmore, Kentucky. God provided me with a Methodist circuit of four churches where I served as student pastor. Every week I drove the round trip of two hundred miles to serve my churches.

For this each of them gave me five dollars a week and I was able to eat bountifully each weekend.

By squeezing everything I could into the schedule, I completed the three-year seminary in two years. At last I had made it to my goal. I was a minister! I had worked so long and so hard that I didn't quite know how to stop. But this was it; this was what God had called me to do. I was sent to the Methodist church in Claypool, Indiana, for my first full-time assignment. I threw myself into the work with all the zeal I could muster, and slowly the three churches in the circuit began to grow. The offerings increased, the attendance grew and my salary went up.

Young people accepted Christ in growing numbers, and my flock accepted and loved me and put up with the blunders of a young minister.

Still I felt a growing restlessness within me. There was a void, an emptiness, almost a boredom. Increasingly, my thoughts were drawn toward the Army chaplaincy. I knew the soldier, his thoughts and his temptations. Did God want me to serve the men in uniform? I prayed about it. "I'll go if You want me to go, Lord; I'll stay if You want me to stay. . . ."

Gradually the pull toward the Army got stronger. In 1953 I volunteered for the chaplaincy and was accepted. It couldn't have happened if I hadn't received that presidential pardon. God had known and blessed me in this special way.

After three months at chaplains' school, I was sent to join the airborne troopers at Fort Campbell, Kentucky.

At the first opportunity, I boarded an airplane and heard the familiar words: "Get ready; stand up; hook up; stand in the door. . .GO."

I felt the thrust of the wind and the shock as the parachute opened. It still felt like a ten-ton truck hitting me. I was back where I belonged!

3

The Search

It's exciting to be a chaplain, and it was excitement I'd been looking for. I went everywhere with the men. In the air, on the ground, climbing mountains, going on marches, undergoing physical conditioning. In the billets, offices, on the field, or in the mess hall - everywhere I had opportunities to tell men what God wanted to do for them.

I enjoyed every minute of the physical hardships. On jungle-expert training in Panama we all lived in and lived off the fruits of the jungle. The steaming jungle rapidly took its toll, and some men had to be carried out on stretchers. I learned how comfortable it can be to lie in a puddle of mud!

At Fort Campbell I had the opportunity to become a pilot, something I'd always wanted. With a friend I bought an old airplane held together mainly by chewing gum and rubber bands, it seemed. The plane had no radio equipment and we had to fly by sight or instinct. Once I got completely lost and suddenly found myself escorted by two Army planes. They motioned for me to land, and I found I'd been flying over Fort Knox, Kentucky. The angry security police informed me I was lucky not to have been shot down.

Our flying came to an abrupt end when my partner crashlanded the plane in a cornfield.

While stationed at Fort Bragg, North Carolina, I went with the 82nd Airborne Division to the Dominican Republic. This was a small police action, but thirty-nine paratroopers were lost.

Back at Fort Bragg, I continued parachuting and finally received the coveted Army award of Master Parachutist.

From outward appearances all was well. My life was full and exciting and I was doing God's work. Maybe that was part of the problem. I was doing God's work. I didn't like to admit it, but I often became too tense when I talked to the men about God's love for them. Converting them was my business and I struggled hard.

I was always aware that I was falling woefully short of the perfection I longed for. Somehow it was always just beyond the horizon.

As a young boy I'd heard my mother and grandmother talk about the need for purity and holiness in living. They were Wesleyan and Free Methodist and spoke of the work of the Holy Spirit in the life of the Christian.

Whatever it was, I certainly lacked it. I read books about the deeper life of prayer, and went to camp meetings to hear others preach about the power of God.

I didn't see much of that power in my own life, and I desperately longed for it. I wanted to be used of God, and everywhere I looked were people in need. I just didn't have what it took to meet their needs.

A friend gave me a book about an eastern cult claiming to know the method of opening people's minds to the power of God. I learned to lie on a board with my feet elevated and to practice silent meditation.

I began to read everything I could find about psychic phenomena, hypnotism, and spiritism, hoping to find a clue to the secret of letting God's Spirit work in and through me.

About this time I went to Korea and there, in an accident, my glasses shattered into my right eye. Sixty percent of the vision in that eye was gone. The cornea was scarred, and the doctors said vision would never return.

Now, where was the power of God? Christ had walked the earth and healed the blind. He said that greater things even than He had done, those who followed after Him would do.

I went to Seoul twice for eye operations. The verdict was negative. I prayed. Everything in me rebelled against accepting a God of salvation, a God who is omnipotent creator, a God whose name I preach to men who face death on the battlefield, as a God without the power to heal. But where was the key? How was that power released through men? I had to know.

On my third flight to Seoul for a visit to the surgeon, I was sitting in the airplane when suddenly there was a strong sensation within me. It wasn't an audible voice, but something definitely communicated, saying: "Your eyes are going to be all right."

I knew God had spoken. He had spoken to me, just as clearly as He did that Sunday evening in the barn back in Pennsylvania.

The surgeon in Seoul shook his head and said: "Sorry, Chaplain, there's nothing we can do for your eye." Instead of feeling discouragement, I was elated. God had spoken; I trusted Him.

A few months later I had a sudden urge to go back to the doctor to check on my eye. After the examination he looked astonished. "I don't understand," he said. "Your eye is perfectly well."

God had done it! I was thrilled and more determined than ever to research every avenue of contact with His power.

I returned to the United States in 1963, went back to Chaplains' School for six months and was assigned to Fort Bragg, N.C., in 1964.

Here I continued studying hypnosis with renewed vigor, and got involved in the Spiritual Frontiers movement led by Arthur Ford. I had heard that many ministers were drawn to this movement. In Arthur Ford's home I saw firsthand evidence of the workings of a spirit world completely separate from our known rational world. I was fascinated.

But was it scriptural? There were pangs of nagging doubts in the back of my mind. The spirits were unquestionably real, but the Bible speaks of spirits other than God's Holy Spirit, and talks about spiritual wickedness in high places (Ephesians 6). The Bible calls these spirits our enemies, Satan's own forces, and warns us to test all spirits to be sure we aren't being manipulated by the enemy. Satan can cleverly counterfeit the work of the Holy Spirit.

I felt reasonably sure that I wasn't getting myself into a blind alley. These spirits, and the people I met in the movement, did, after all, speak very highly of Christ. They certainly recognized Him as the Son of God and a great spiritual leader who worked many miracles.

The goal for us, they taught, is to become like Christ in all things, since we are also sons of God.

I traveled many miles to talk with people who knew something about the subject, studied books on hypnotism, spoke to doctors, even wrote the Library of Congress. For here, I felt, was the avenue I, as mortal man, could use to help others.

I didn't know I was on dangerous ground. Subtly, but surely, I had begun to look at Jesus Christ as someone much like myself. Someone I could be like if I tried hard enough.

I had greatly underestimated the powers of the enemy. I didn't know it then, but hypnosis is potentially very dangerous spiritually, leaving the subject wide-open for impulses from the realm of Satan.

Oh yes, I was also falling into the trap of thinking of Satan as a bad character with horns from a realm of imagery. He certainly couldn't pose a threat to the sophisticated man of the twentieth century.

C.S. Lewis once said that Satan's cleverest trick is to convince the world that he doesn't exist.

My faith had become damaged and seriously undermined, although I didn't know it yet. The change was so subtle. Perhaps the fine line was crossed when I found myself talking about Jesus as teacher and miracle worker and failing to mention that He died on a cross for us, that His blood cleanses us from sin.

Satan quoted Scriptures even in Jesus' time. He still does, and really doesn't mind when we do. But he would like to see us forget about the cross, the blood, and the resurrected Jesus.

Paul speaks about the secret of the Christian life in Colossians 1:27. The secret is Christ in us. Not that we become like Him, but that He lives in us and transforms us from within. Others may look at us and say we appear to be Christlike, but not because we have become more worthy or holy or spiritual or pure. He lives in us. That's the secret.

The subtle danger of the so-called, "Christian Spiritualist Movement" or "Spiritual Frontiers Movement" is that it would lead men to try to copy Christ and appropriate spiritual powers for themselves, and so commit the original sin of Satan, the fallen angel, who wanted to be like God Himself.

Without Christ as Savior, without the cross, there would be no plan of salvation, no possible way to be forgiven of sin. In fact, there would be no gospel.

I was falling into the trap. My motives were pure; I honestly wanted power to help others overcome their problems and their sicknesses of body and mind.

It took an act of God to open my eyes to the error of my ways.

4

Be Filled

For some time I had been going to a small weekly prayer group near Fort Bragg. One evening, Ruth, a member of the group, was visibly moved during a prayer session. I had watched her during several meetings and often thought I would like to ask her how she had come to experience such obvious joy in her life. Unlike some of the rest of us, she seemed to be filled continuously with a joy I certainly had felt only on rare occasions in my life.

This particular evening Ruth confided in me: "I was so blessed I almost prayed out loud in tongues!"

"You almost what?" I was horrified.

"Prayed in tongues," Ruth said brightly.

I lowered my voice and looked around to see if we were being watched. "Ruth, you could have ruined our group! Whatever has come over you?"

Ruth laughed heartily. "I've been praying in tongues ever since I received the Baptism in the Holy Spirit."

"What is that?" I'd never heard the term before.

Ruth patiently explained that it was the same experience that the disciples had at Pentecost. "I experienced my own Pentecost." She smiled with unmistakable radiance.

"I thought you were Baptist." I felt shaken.

"I am, but God is moving in all denominations."

I had heard rumors of a wave of emotionalism invading the churches, people getting off on fads and losing faith in Christ. I had heard some tales about Pentecostals being "drunk in the spirit," whatever that meant, and having wild orgies. I knew Ruth needed help badly.

I put my hand on her arm. "Be careful, Ruth," I said earnestly. "You're playing with dangerous stuff. I'll be praying for you, and if you need help, call me."

Ruth smiled and patted my hand. "Thank you, Merlin. I appreciate your concern."

Some time later she called me.

"Merlin, a group called Camp Farthest Out is having a retreat at Morehead City. We'd like you to go." It sounded like something I'd better stay away from. I tactfully replied that I would go if I could, which meant that I wouldn't be able to.

Within the next week several others called. A businessman reminded me that I would need my golf clubs. A lady from Raleigh telephoned to tell me that she had arranged for all my expenses to be paid if I would go. Someone else called to say I could bring another minister free of charge. This was too much. How could I resist all this genuine interest in my spiritual well-being? I said, "Thank you, I'll go."

I got in touch with a Presbyterian minister friend and invited him to come along. He hedged.

33

"It's an all-expenses-paid trip at a resort hotel!"

"I'll go."

On the way Dick said: "Merlin, why are we going to this thing?"

"I don't know," I said. "But it's for free, so let's enjoy it."

In the hotel lobby we were greeted with such warm enthusiasm from people we'd never seen that I was beginning to wonder what kind of strange beings we had fallen amongst.

The services were unlike anything we'd ever attended. People sang with uninhibited joy, clapped their hands, and actually raised their arms while they were singing.

Both Dick and I felt very much out of place, but agreed there was a joy here from which we could learn something.

One very cultured and refined-looking lady kept coming up to us and saying: "Has anything happened yet?"

"No, ma'am, what do you mean?" we'd answer.

"You'll see, you'll see," she always said.

Ruth and some of the others who had invited us urged me to have a private talk with a certain lady who they said had unusual power.

They took us to meet her, and I instantly disliked her. She quoted Scripture in a way that made me feel as if she was trying to convert me. I didn't like to have Scripture quoted to me, with what seemed to be a judgmental attitude.

Still, our friends insisted that we have a talk with her, and since they'd paid our way there, I felt we ought to oblige.

We sat patiently as she told us what God had done in her life and in the lives of others that she knew. She made numerous references to the "Baptism in the Holy Spirit," and went through the Scriptures to show that the experience had been a common one for Christians in the first century.

"The Holy Spirit is still doing the same thing in many people's lives today," she said. "Jesus Christ still baptizes those who believe in Him, just as He did at Pentecost."

I felt a twinge of excitement. Could it be that I could experience my own Pentecost? Could I see tongues of fire, hear the rush of wind, and speak in an unknown tongue?

She had finished talking and sat looking at us.

"I'd like to pray for you," she said softly. "That you might receive the Baptism in the Holy Spirit."

Without hesitating I said, "Yes."

She placed her hands on my head and began to pray softly. I waited for "it" to hit me. Nothing happened. I didn't feel a thing.

She went on and placed her hands on Dick's head. When she had finished praying I looked at him and he looked at me. I could tell he hadn't felt anything either. This whole thing was a fake.

The lady looked at us both with a hint of a smile.

"You haven't felt anything yet, have you?"

We shook our heads. "No, ma'am."

"I'm going to pray for you in a language you will not understand. As I pray you will receive a new language of your own."

35

Again she placed her hands on my head. I felt nothing, saw nothing, heard nothing. When she was through praying, she asked if I could hear or sense any words within me that I didn't understand. I thought for a minute and realized that there were in my mind words that didn't mean anything to me. I felt certain that these strange words were strictly a product of my own imagination, and I told her so.

"If you said them out loud, would you feel as if you were being made a fool of?" she asked.

"I certainly would."

"Would you be willing to be a fool for Christ's sake?" This put the whole situation in a different perspective. Of course I'd do anything for Christ, but speaking out loud such utter nonsense could mean disaster for my future. I could imagine all those people going around telling everyone that a Methodist chaplain had been praying in an unknown tongue. I might even have to leave the Army! Still, what if this was what Christ wanted me to do? Suddenly even my Army career seemed less important. Haltingly I began to speak out loud the words that were forming in my mind.

Still I felt nothing different. I did believe that Jesus Christ had given me a new tongue as a sign that He had baptized me in the Holy Spirit, yet the disciples at Pentecost had acted like drunk men. Obviously they had been overwhelmed by some feeling.

I watched Dick; his experience seemed to be the same as mine. He spoke words of an unknown language and believed in the validity of it, yet displayed no emotional reaction.

"Your experience is based on faith in a fact, not on feeling," said the lady, apparently reading our minds.

I sat in deep thought. I didn't *feel* any different, but *was* I different? I looked up; an amazing realization had just hit me.

"I once again *know* that Jesus Christ is alive!" I said. "I don't just believe, I KNOW!"

Why, of course! The Holy Spirit brings witness of Jesus Christ, says the Bible. Now I knew that to be a fact. That was the source of the new authority of the disciples after Pentecost. They didn't remember a man who had lived and died and risen again. They *knew* Him in the present tense because He had filled them with His Holy Spirit whose primary purpose is to witness to Jesus Christ!

Even as I saw the magnitude of my sin, I also saw Jesus Christ in all His splendor as my redeemer. I saw Him for what I'd always known deep in my heart that He was. All of my recent nagging doubts were swept away by a wave of joyous certainty. It was glorious! Never again could I doubt that Jesus Christ was who He said He was. Never again could I commit the folly of thinking that He had been a mere man, a good man, an example for us to follow.

What a marvelous truth: Jesus Christ living in us; His power operating through us. He is the vine. His life pulsates through our beings.

We are nothing apart from Him, can do nothing in our own power.

"Thank you, Jesus!" I stood up, and as I reached my full height, something hit me! I was suddenly filled and overflowing with a feeling of warmth and love for everybody in the room.

It must have hit Dick at the same time. I saw the tears well up in his eyes, and without a word we reached out and gave each other a bear hug, laughing and crying at the same time.

I looked at the dear lady I had resented so fiercely just a short while ago, and realized that I loved her. She was my sister in Christ!

We went downstairs for lunch, and I felt an overwhelming love for everyone I saw. I had never known anything like it.

That evening Dick and I began to pray in one of the rooms. People came in to join us and soon the room was full. As we prayed, others were filled with the Holy Spirit. The hotel rang with shouts of joy as people experienced the fullness of Christ's presence.

At 2:00 a.m. Dick and I tried to go to sleep. It was no use; we were too excited.

I said: "Dick, let's get up and pray some more." We prayed another two hours for everyone we knew, and then praised God for His goodness to us.

5

His Power Within You

I returned to Fort Bragg anxious to share with everyone the wonderful thing that had happened to me. I had once wondered how an experience like this would affect my ministry. How well I remembered my own reaction to the "Pentecostal emotionalism" in the church.

Now I knew that whatever the reaction, I would not be able to keep from sharing what I had experienced.

The first day I went to our headquarters company orderly room. The First Sergeant was sitting behind his desk. He was big and rough and well known for his gruff manners.

"First Sergeant," I said, "did I ever tell you that Jesus loves you?"

To my amazement the tears began to roll down his cheeks.

He said: "No, Chaplain, you never told me anything like that."

I felt my face flush hot with shame. For over a year I had seen him several times a day and I had never told him anything about Jesus.

I walked into the hallway and met the Supply Sergeant.

"Sergeant, did I ever tell you that Jesus loves you and I love you too?"

"No, Sir, you never told me anything like that."
Again I felt ashamed, and he said: "Sir, do you
have a minute to talk?" We went to my office
and he poured out a host of problems I had
never known he had. When he was through I
asked if he would like to accept Christ as his
Savior. He said he would, and knelt with tears
streaming down his face.

Everywhere I went, men accepted Christ. It
seemed that there was a power in me that was
doing the talking for me. When I started to speak
to someone, I had no idea what I was going to
say, but whatever came had a new power that
drew men to Christ.

It was easy to serve God this way. The old
tension was gone, and I could laugh. Preaching
was no longer something to labor over. It became pure joy just to let His thoughts pour
through me.

All Army personnel must attend a character
guidance class once a month. Teaching this class
as chaplains, we are not allowed to preach. As
carefully as I could, I one day told the class that
the God of our country is still alive and daily answers prayers. After the class a Private came up
to me, and with his nose six inches from mine,
rather insolently said: "You really believe all that
stuff, don't you?"

"Yes, I do," I said.

"Do you mean that if you prayed now, God
would answer?"

"Yes," I said, "I know He will."

"Do you think it is wrong to smoke?"

The question was an unexpected one. "For some it may be wrong, for others right," I said evasively.

"I've been smoking since I was fourteen," the Private said. "Now I smoke three packs a day, and the doctor told me this morning that if I don't stop, it will kill me."

I said: "There's no question about it; for you it is wrong to smoke."

"Then you ask your God to make me quit!"

How could I pray like that? The obvious pat answers were swirling through my head: God helps those who help themselves, or he could pray that God would help him want to quit. But that wasn't what he'd asked me.

"God," I prayed silently, "help me know what to do."

Immediately I felt a strong impression: "Pray in your new language!"

"Out loud?"

"No, just silently."

I began to pray in the language I had received at the retreat. Then I paused.

There came another impression: "Put your hand on his shoulder and pray."

I obediently put my hand on his shoulder. "Pray what?"

"Silently pray in your new language." I did. Then came the impression again: "Translate it into English."

Without thinking, I opened my mouth and out came the words: "God, don't let him smoke again as long as he lives."

What a prayer! If the man ever smoked again he'd be convinced that God didn't answer prayer. I felt utterly confused, and just turned on my heels and left.

In the days that followed, I asked God repeatedly if I had misunderstood. Would my mistake make that man disbelieve? Again and again came the impression: "Just trust me."

Trusting God apparently meant going out on a limb without anything to hold onto but faith. With new eagerness I dove into an intensive study of God's Word. If I was going to operate on faith, it would have to be faith in the integrity and very nature of God. I had to know Him, and I found that the more I read, the stronger I believed. Bible reading had never been this exciting before. From the pages rose a new knowledge of God the omnipotent who promised that we could do all things in Christ. Who said that the power within us is the same power that raised Christ from the dead!

In Ephesians 3:20-21 Paul wrote: "Now to him who by his power within us is able to do infinitely more than we ever dare to ask or imagine - to him be glory in the Church and in Christ Jesus forever and ever, amen! (J.B. Phillips translation)

Carefully, I studied Paul's instructions to the church at Corinth. He listed the various ways the Holy Spirit was known to operate through men: there were speaking in tongues, interpretation of tongues, healing, miracles, prophesying, preaching, wisdom, knowledge, faith, discernment.

How could I know what "gifts" God wanted to express through me? Had He given me any special gifts?

Again the verse from Ephesians came back to me: "He who by His power within us." No, I didn't have any gifts. All I could do was to be willing to let God operate through me.

In other words, my job was strictly that of being obedient to the impressions or urgings I felt within me. The Scripture says that He could do far more than we dare ask or imagine. Obviously, there was no way I could anticipate or know what God wanted to do.

One evening in our prayer group, I talked about God's power to heal our bodies. One lady spoke up. "Why don't you ask God to heal one of us then?"

I felt a bit shaky. Of course I knew God could and would hear prayer for the sick. But would He hear and answer me?

"Okay," I said, with a sudden release of faith. "Who wants to be prayed for?"

"I do," said the same lady. "One of my eyes has been weeping tears for several months. Medication hasn't helped. Please pray about it."

I held my breath, placed my hands on her head, and prayed, mustering all my faith to believe that God was healing her right then. When I was through, her eye was still weeping. Had I done something wrong? Again came the prompting within. "Trust Me." All right, faith means believing something you don't see. All the stories I'd read in the Bible had made it very plain; the difference between victory and defeat was always a matter of faith. God couldn't do a thing when the Israelites refused to believe. The promises in the Bible are plentiful to those who will only believe.

"Thank you, Lord," I said out loud, "for hearing our prayer."

That night the lady called me, "Chaplain, guess what happened?" Her voice was bubbling with excitement.

"Tell me!"

"I was sitting here reading when I suddenly realized that something had happened to my eye. It is completely healed!"

I was thrilled. "Thank you, Lord," I said, "I get your point. I'll do the trusting; You'll do the rest."

A local Presbyterian minister who had been filled with the Holy Spirit had been reluctant to tell his congregation. He invited a member of our prayer group to give her testimony during a Sunday evening service, and several of us in the group came along to be in prayer.

As she told how she, a Southern Baptist, had been baptized in the Holy Spirit, there was dead silence in the church. It was evident that God was speaking to the people. At the close of the service the pastor called on me to pronounce the benediction. I stood up, but instead of giving the benediction, I began to speak the very first words that came into my mind: "Everyone who wants to come to the altar and surrender his life to God, please come forward."

Dead silence! There had never been an altar call in the history of that church. Then one by one, people began to come forward, falling on their knees.

I walked over to the first one. I didn't know what to pray. I didn't know why he had come forward. I bowed my head. Within me I prayed silently: "Show me how to pray, God." I heard "Pray in the Spirit." I silently prayed in my new language.

"Now begin to translate what you have said."

"Lord, forgive this man for his drunkenness, his dishonesty in business." I was shocked at my own words. What if I had misunderstood? I could really mess things up for my minister friend.

I walked over to the next person and followed the same procedure. "Lord, forgive this man for his vile temper, his ugly disposition, and his selfish treatment of his family."

I went from one to another, and with my hands on the person's head prayed as I was prompted to pray, prayers of repentance and confession.

By the time I was through I knew I had really crawled way out on a limb in complete trust.

After the benediction the people came to me one by one. With tears of joy they said: "You prayed for exactly what I needed, but how did you know my problem?"

Days later the minister told me that the congregation had been revolutionized. Many of the people who had come forward that night were elders and officers in the church. Now the entire congregation was overflowing with enthusiasm, zeal, and joy.

I felt like shouting. I hadn't known the problems that beset the men and women of that church, but God had. He knows the heart and mind of all of us, and can speak through us in a power that will directly minister to the exact needs of every individual. If people respond, it isn't our doing, but His. If they refuse, again we do not get blamed for a failure.

Every day and wherever I went it was the same; people responding to Jesus Christ. Whenever I fell back into the habit of trying to think beforehand what I would say to someone, the results were immediate. I became tense; the power and presence of God simply didn't flow. The principle of letting go and letting God was valid. All I had to do was relax in the presence of God, letting my mind go blank and opening my mouth in faith to speak whatever God impressed on me. Always the words spoke directly to a need, always the person was wonderfully helped.

I marveled. I had been a pastor for many years and worked hard at it, yet I had never seen so much happen in the lives of so many in the short time since Jesus Christ invaded my being in the fullness of His Spirit.

Without the pressures of having to preplan and organize and research and write sermon notes, I found that I had much more time to spend in Bible reading and prayer. It seemed as if I suddenly had more energy than ever before, and I never had the frustrating experience of wasting time on projects that turned out to be ineffective.

As long as I rested in Christ, it seemed that God took my days, and every detail, every appointment, every happening began to fall into place in a perfect whole. No longer did I experience confusion and conflicts of appointments or schedules.

My only regret was that I had not discovered this experience of yielding myself fully to God many years before.

About this time, Oral Roberts came to Fayetteville. A huge tent was set up, and night after night thousands came to hear him preach and pray for the sick. I wanted to meet him personally so I found out which local minister would be in charge of the service. I went to see him and volunteered to do anything I could to help.

He was amazed that a Methodist chaplain would want to be involved. He had never been able to get anyone but Pentecostal ministers to assist before.

From the opening night, I was on the platform in uniform. I was there next to Oral Roberts as he prayed for the sick, and I saw physical changes take place as bodies were healed! What a tremendous joy!

My chaplain friends began to hint that if I continued appearing in such places and being associated with men like Oral Roberts, I might as well forget about ever "getting anyplace" in the Army chaplaincy. They were probably right, but

I'd rather be obedient to God and see His power clearly demonstrated than be seeking the temporal approval of men.

The next week I was casually leafing through a list of chaplains who had been selected for promotion to Lieutenant Colonel. I hadn't been a Major long enough to be considered, but there, on the list, was my name! Later I found that the Army has the authority to promote five percent of its officers before they are eligible under the ordinary rules.

All I could think was, "Thank You, Lord, for showing me that I can trust You to look after all my needs."

Obedience sometimes meant going against the expressed wishes of the people who came to ask for help.

A young Army Lieutenant brought his wife to see me. "She would like prayer for the Baptism in the Holy Spirit," he said.

I had a most unusual feeling within. I just knew that this girl had already received this experience. She hadn't said a word since they entered my office, yet I knew this was so.

I said: "You have already received the Baptism so you don't need to be prayed for again."

"How do you know that?" She looked surprised. "I've tried to believe ever since I was prayed for."

"I know because the Holy Spirit tells me," I said. "He also says that before you stand up you will receive the evidence of speaking in a new tongue.

This was really way-out, I thought. What if nothing happened? Her faith would surely be shaken. Yet within I felt a certainty. I invited both of them to join me in a prayer of thanksgiving for what God had already done.

Before I finished, I could hear her softly praying in her new language. She was so filled with joy that she nearly floated out of the office.

One day a young Private showed up in my office. I remembered the prayer I'd prayed for him: "God, don't let him ever smoke again." He was beaming all over his face.

"Sir," he burst out, "You'll never believe what happened to me after you left."

I'd seen enough amazing happenings in the last month to believe anything.

"Yes, I'll believe," I said. "Tell me."

"When you turned and left, I laughed and thought, *This will be easy. All I have to do is smoke, and I'll prove that God doesn't answer prayer.* I went into the latrine and lit up a cigarette, took a big drag, and immediately started to vomit. I figured that was a coincidence, probably something I ate, and later that afternoon I tried smoking again. The same thing happened. For the next three days, every time I tried to smoke I vomited. Now, if I just think about smoking I feel like vomiting."

I was overjoyed. Jesus Christ promised that the Holy Spirit would be with us to guide us into all truth. I hadn't misunderstood His instructions.

A few days later the Private came back.

"Sir, would you pray one more prayer for me?"

"I surely will!"

"Please pray that God will forgive my sins and help me to accept Christ as my Savior."

Within minutes we were on our knees together and he joyfully accepted Christ.

Months later I told about this incident in the First Baptist Church of Columbus, Georgia. After the service a man came up to me and said: "I was in Admin Company of the 82nd Airborne Division when that happened. That man was going all over the company telling about the chaplain who had fixed him so he couldn't smoke!"

What a wonderful truth! Not only does God save, He means business when He says He can remold us and make us into His image. He can literally take away our old habits and hang-ups and impure thoughts and renew us from within!

I had received the Baptism in the Holy Spirit only a couple of months ago, yet it seemed I'd already lived a lifetime in this new dimension.

Now I was in for an encounter with the enemy in force. I was suddenly the victim of an unusual affliction. All my life I'd been strong as a horse in top physical condition. Now every time I exerted myself in the least, my heart began to beat rapidly. I was weak and ached all over. Reluctantly I went to bed for a week. My condition didn't improve at all. I went to the hospital to see what the medical verdict would be, and they immediately slapped me on a stretcher and hustled me off to bed. Test after test gave no clue to what ailed me. I felt wretched, weak, and in pain, and it seemed to get worse instead of better. At this rate I'd just as soon be dead. All my energies seemed depleted, and the outlook was bleak.

Then suddenly one night when I wondered if the end might be near, there was the strong impression: "Do you still trust me?

"Yes, Lord." I whispered it into the darkened room. A quiet peace began to move through me, and I fell into a deep sleep.

The next morning I felt much better. The doctors insisted I stay in bed for a while, and I was grateful for days of prayer, praise, and study.

One day I was reading one of Glenn Clark's books, and I suddenly felt the voice within me ask: "Will you now live like Jesus?"

I could only answer: "Yes, Lord."

"But what about your thoughts and desires. Are they pure?"

"No, Lord."

"Do you want them to be?"

"Oh, yes, Lord. All my life I've struggled to overcome impure thoughts and desires."

"Will you give me all your impure thoughts?"

"Yes, Lord."

"Forever?"

"Oh yes, Lord. Forever."

Suddenly it was as if a heaviness had been lifted from me, as if a mist had parted and everything looked clean and pure. The door to the ward opened and a young nurse walked through. I followed her with my eyes. She was a beautiful young nurse, and all I could think was: "What a beautiful child of God." There was not even a fleeting thought of temptation!

Back home from the hospital, I went to our prayer group and felt a strong impression to ask them to pray for me. I had always been the one to pray for others. Now I sat in the chair in the center of the group, and they prepared to pray for me. "What do you want us to ask God to do?"

I thought for a moment. "Ask God to use me more than ever," I said. They began to pray, and suddenly, in the Spirit, I saw Jesus kneeling before me. He was holding my feet and resting His head on my knees. He said: "I don't want to use you. I want you to use Me!"

It was as if a door had opened into a new understanding of Jesus. He told the disciples that they had to permit Him to kneel before them while He washed their feet. He wants to give Himself for us each moment of our lives just as completely as He gave Himself on the cross. We have nothing to give Him; we have only to receive of Him!

6

Vietnam

In 1966 I received orders to go to Vietnam with the 80th General Support Group, then stationed at Fort Bragg.

We boarded ship in San Francisco, and as we left the bay moving out to sea, I stood at the railing feeling the peace of God within me and around me. This was His will for me, I knew.

On board I immediately started a prayer group, a Bible study, and regular worship services. We spent twenty-one days at sea and each day several men accepted Christ.

The devil would frequently whisper in my ear that they were just doing it because they were going to Vietnam and their decisions weren't really honest.

Months later I had proof of how much of a liar the devil is. Many of the men who made decisions for Christ were with a unit that left us as soon as we reached Vietnam. One day I walked into their unit, and one of the Sergeants saw me. He almost exploded with joy. "Praise the Lord, Chaplain Carothers."

He told me of all the things God had been doing. Together we went to see others in the unit who had accepted Christ aboard ship, and they

53

told me about the Bible classes they were holding and of the men they had led to Christ.

"Do you remember Lieutenant Stover?" they asked.

"Yes, I do." I remembered the afternoon he stood on deck and told me how he had been running from God all through college. He had given his life back to Christ right there and told me that as soon as he got out of the Army he would answer the call to full time ministry.

"He has started a tremendous choir and the men really enjoy singing with him."

They took me to meet the Lieutenant and we had a joyful reunion.

As soon as I arrived in Cam Rahn Bay I organized a Saturday night prayer group. Soon there were twenty-five men meeting each week. I began by challenging them to believe that God would answer our prayers if we would just believe Him.

For several weeks I asked for specific prayer requests. Finally one evening a Warrant Officer spoke up.

"Well, Sir, I sure would be pleased for you to pray for my wife. We have been married six years and she is so against religion that she won't even let us have prayer at the table. I don't think it will do much good to pray for her, but I'd be glad for you to try."

I thought this was an unusual request to start with, but I was learning that God knows His business. I asked the men to hold hands in a circle, and we began praying for our first miracle.

None of the men had ever tried believing for a miracle, but they were willing to try. I had been sharing with them all the wonderful things God had been doing in my life since I received the Baptism in the Holy Spirit.

Near the battlefront in Vietnam they were far from the distractions at home and ready to start grasping the deeper things of the Spirit.

Two weeks later the Warrant Officer came to the prayer group with a letter in his hand. Tears flowed down his face as he read the letter to us:

"Darling, you will probably find it difficult to believe what has been happening here at home. One week ago I was standing at our kitchen sink on a Saturday morning. I began to have a most unusual experience. A big white sign began flashing through my mind. On it in big black letters was the word 'REVIVAL.' I couldn't get it out of my mind. No matter what I tried to think about, the sign stayed in front of me all morning long. By noon I was really upset. I called your sister and asked her if there was a big revival sign some place in town. I thought I might have seen it. She said there was no such sign, but they were having revival at their church. 'Would you like to come?' she asked me.

I said, 'You know I never go to such things.' But the sign stayed with me and by evening it was so strong that I called your sister and asked if I could go with her. During the service an invitation was given and I went forward. I've waited a week to write you about this for I wanted to be sure that I really was giving my life to Christ. But Darling, it is true! I was baptized today, and I am thrilled! I can't wait for you to come home so we can have a real Christian home."

"Chaplain," said the officer, "do you know what time it was here when it was Saturday morning at home?"

I shook my head.

"Saturday night when we prayed for her. That's when she began to see the sign. And do you remember Sunday morning?"

"Yes, I remember." He had come forward when the invitation had been given at the close of the morning worship service. I had said that I thought he already was a Christian and he answered: "Yes, I am, Sir, but I was standing back there and got the strongest feeling that if I came forward it would somehow help my wife."

Now he looked at me, tears flowing freely. "Chaplain, do you realize what time that was back home?"

Then it dawned on me. It had been Saturday night. The night his wife accepted Christ. An electric thrill went through our prayer group. Tears rolled down many cheeks. The men were learning for themselves that God does answer prayer.

Sitting next to the Warrant Officer was a black Sergeant. I could see that he was deeply troubled. "What's wrong?" I asked.

"Sir, my wife is like his; she won't accept any kind of religion in our home. I've been realizing that if I had just a little faith two weeks ago we could have prayed for my wife too, and maybe the same thing would have happened to her."

What a coincidence! Far away in Vietnam were two soldiers with the same unusual problem. "Let's pray for your wife right now," I said with enthusiasm.

"Sir, I believe I missed my chance. I just don't have faith to pray now."

"You don't need to depend on your faith alone," I said. "Just believe in our prayers, and we will have faith for you."

We joined hands and began to pray. There was a new fervor among the men. They had begun to see for themselves that God hears and God answers.

The next morning I was in my office when the Sergeant came bouncing in with a letter in his hand and a big smile.

"Don't tell me you got an answer already," I said jokingly.

"I sure did!"

He was nearly in orbit and suddenly the words flashed into my mind: "Before they call I will answer." Could it be?

"What does the letter say?"

It was nearly a duplication of the one we had heard the night before. The Sergeant's wife also had been saved, baptized, and was already teaching a Sunday School class.

"Oh, God," I breathed, "I love You, I love You, I love You!"

One Saturday night a new officer came to our meeting. He was obviously not in sympathy with our approach to prayer.

"Chaplain, if God is actually answering prayer, why doesn't He do something important?"

"What would you consider important?" I asked quietly.

"From the first day our little son was able to stand up, he would look at his feet and cry out in pain. We have taken him to every doctor and specialist in the area. We have had special shoes, casts, braces, wrappings, and nothing helps. He is seven years old now and every night my wife has to put his feet on a pillow and rub them before he can go to sleep. Why doesn't God do something for him?"

Under my breath I asked God to show me how to pray; then I said: "We will pray and God will heal him!" I felt very certain. "You don't believe, but we do, and God will heal him. Join the circle with us and let's pray."

The men prayed with renewed hunger to see God move. Here was a third request for someone back home. I knew God had sent it.

Two weeks later another letter arrived:

Dear:

I've waited for a week to tell you about something that is almost too good to be true. One week ago I noticed that for the first time in his life, Paul didn't mention his feet once during the day. He went to sleep that night without a pillow under his feet. I wanted to write to you right away, but was afraid of raising your hopes. The next day it was the same. It's been a whole week now, and he hasn't complained about his feet hurting!"

"Chaplain, it's hard for me to believe," said the officer, struggling to hold back the tears. "But the day my boy's feet stopped hurting is the day we prayed for him!"

For months afterward, every time I saw this officer, he would raise his arms and say, "His feet don't hurt yet!"

From then on our men began to grow in faith. More and more prayers were answered. Other men came to our group to hear about the amazing things that were going on. I began to read letters and reports of answered prayers from the pulpit Sunday mornings, and daily men would wave to me and yell, "Any new miracles, Chaplain?"

Often I called back: "The greatest miracle of all; another man has accepted Christ and received eternal life!"

As the Spirit of the Lord moved among us, many men were drawn to Christ.

One Sunday morning I had given an invitation to accept Christ, and many had come forward to pray. After the service I went into my office to spend a few minutes alone with the Lord. I was preparing to leave when a Sergeant suddenly burst through the doorway and fell on his knees in the middle of the floor.

"Please, pray for me," he cried in obvious anguish.

He then began to confess sins of immorality, addiction to alcohol and drugs, neglect of his children and wife. He poured out his sorrow with tears of repentance. When he was through, I told him how God loved him and had sent Jesus Christ to die on the cross for every one of the sins he had confessed. "All you have to do is accept Christ as your Savior, and God will give you eternal life and complete pardon," I said.

"I do, I do," he sobbed, and a smile of peace and joy flooded his face as he began to thank and praise God.

Later he told me what had brought him running to my office. Earlier that morning he had walked by the chapel on his way to the post exchange. Suddenly he felt an urge to step inside. "This is crazy," he thought, "I haven't been inside a church for six years; I don't have any reason to go now." He went on to the PX, but something kept pulling him back. Finally he decided to go to the chapel where the service was just then getting underway. He sat through it all and when the congregation stood up to sing the last hymn he realized he was shaking so badly that he couldn't stand without holding on to the chair in front of him.

He was afraid that at any moment he would fall to the floor, and he felt a powerful urge to walk to the front and give his life to God.

"I just can't," he told himself and began to leave the chapel. Outside in the street his legs began to give way and he knew that he wouldn't be able to stand up much longer. A voice inside told him that now was the time. He must obey God or else God would let him die. Without waiting any longer he turned and ran back to the chapel and burst through my doorway.

One of our chaplains was a Southern Baptist. We were good friends and he loved the Lord, but he was scared to death of my emphasis on the Holy Spirit. The ideas of faith healing, casting out of demons and evil spirits, being filled with the Holy Spirit, and experiencing the gifts of the Spirit were completely strange to him. He came to one of our prayer groups and then asked to be excused from ever attending another.

He was particularly worried about the way one of us would sit in a chair in the middle of a circle while others would place their hands on him and pray that God would meet his particular needs. He had never seen this done before, and it seemed like something unchristian to him.

Through the men who kept coming to the group, he heard of things happening. Men who were discouraged, defeated, and ready to give up would ask to be prayed for. They told him how they had experienced total release from their burdens. After sitting in the chair and having others pray for them with the laying on of hands, they had been filled with a peace and joy that stayed with them. They told how Christ had become more real to them from that moment on.

Little by little, these things were affecting the chaplain. He began to realize that God works in many ways, even in ways much different from what he had seen and experienced before. Then something unexpected happened.

A chaplain in another front line unit was killed. My friend was called to take his place immediately. He felt naturally a little apprehensive and came to my office to say goodbye. Hesitantly, he confessed that the ministry through our prayer group had come to mean a great deal to him. Then he knelt on the floor with tears flowing. He took my hands and placed them on his head.

"Merlin, please pray for me the way you pray."

Quietly I began to pray for him in tongues, and as I prayed he began to be filled with joy and peace. Laughing through tears he told me how all his fears were gone. He was ready to go into the battle lines.

A few weeks later he called me to say that he had been nearly killed in a helicopter accident the first day he arrived in his unit.

"Even then I could only feel an overflowing love and trust in Jesus Christ," he said.

My unit moved north to Chu Lai and joined the Americal Division. We were now in the very thick of the battle along with the Marines. More and more I saw evidences of God's power protecting His children. When we trust Him, no power on earth can touch us unless it is God's will.

On several occasions when I was scheduled to go to certain places I felt a last-minute urge to change my plans. Later I found that each time I obeyed such an urge, I had avoided an incident that could have gotten me killed.

Once I was scheduled to hold a service on a beach for men who were unloading five-hundred-pound bombs. At the last minute I was strongly impressed to cancel the service. At the exact time and place where we would have met, an explosion set off the bombs. If we had gathered there, many of the men would have been killed.

An old friend, Chaplain Burton Hatch, was division chaplain of the Americal Division. He invited me to hold a Sunday evening service, and at the close of the service several men came forward to accept Christ. I prayed with each one of them.

The next morning one of the men came back to the chapel. He looked a mess, with clothes dripping wet and dirty and hair plastered down his forehead. But his face shone and he kept saying: "Praise the Lord; thank you, Jesus!"

Early that morning he and five others had been fully equipped with a combat assault load: hand grenades, bandoliers of bullets around their necks, and heavy flak vests. They boarded the helicopter and headed north along the coast and over the China Sea. The pilot was flying too close to the water, and a sudden large wave hit the skid of the chopper. With a mighty jerk, the helicopter tipped over and dove straight into the sea. Men were thrown in all directions.

The young soldier suddenly realized that he was under water and going down, fast. He tried to swim toward the surface and managed to get a breath of air before going under again, weighted down by the heavy equipment. He tried desperately to free himself, but couldn't. As he began to sink, he told me, he suddenly remembered that he had accepted Christ the evening before. He was ready to die and suddenly was filled with a great peace of heart and mind. It really didn't matter if he couldn't free himself from the heavy gear. Once more he came to the surface and again he sank under. The third time he came up he realized that his strength was gone and he would soon be with his Lord. At that very moment he felt the equipment slide from around him! He came to the surface and was free. He began to swim to shore and there he found that he was the only survivor.

After several months at Chu Lai I was transferred south to Quin Yahn to serve with the 85th Evacuation Hospital. Men who had been wounded only a few hours before were brought to us. Over and over I saw the power of God working. These men were ready to accept Christ. Man after man told me how he had been saved from death by a power beyond his understanding.

"What was it?" I asked.

"I can't explain it," they would say. "All of a sudden, when I knew I was going to die, I became aware of a great power surrounding me. I was then sure I was safe. I knew it was God, and that He didn't want me to die."

Often the men asked me why God had chosen to save them. I told them that He had some special purpose for their lives and He would reveal it as they listened to His voice.

I went from bed to bed talking to the boys and was often overcome with emotion. They were torn, bleeding, and in some cases, dying. But I never heard anyone complain. They were confident that the job they had been doing was important, and that for some reason they were saved from death. I saw nurses turn away in tears as they saw the strength and courage of these men. No matter how great the pain, they would grin and say, "I'm fine."

One night a nurse called me to the hospital to see an Army Major. When he saw me he began to weep. He was covered with bandages, and for ten minutes I stood there while he tried to stop the flow of tears. I wondered what the problem was. Had he been told that his legs would have to be amputated? They were covered by heavy bandages and looked as if they were badly hurt.

Perhaps he had received word that someone at home was seriously ill.

Finally the Major gained control of himself and began to tell me an amazing story.

Just a few hours earlier he had been a passenger in a helicopter. They had been hit by ground fire and crashed into the thick jungle. Six men had been scattered over the side of a mountain. When the Major came to, he realized he was injured too seriously to move. He could hear the cries of other men who were also unable to move. In the distance he could hear rifle shots. The Viet Cong were converging on the position where they had seen the aircraft go down. They were moving in to capture the Americans.

The Major suddenly realized he had reached the end. The VC would not attempt to carry out the wounded Americans. They would probably practice the cruel sport of torturing them to death.

He tried to pray, but realized he didn't know how. He had attended church all his life, but he had never really talked to God. But all at once he "felt" someone say: "Just ask and believe!"

With a burst of anguish, and in new faith he cried: "Oh, God, please help me!" He realized that for the first time in his life he had talked to God. Still, he could hear the VC move in closer.

Miles away, another Army helicopter was flying north. The pilot later told this story: He felt a sudden, overpowering urge to turn and go east. *But why?* he reasoned. His destination was north. Contrary to all military rules he made a ninety-degree turn and headed east. He then felt an even stronger urge to fly lower and slower. This was even less logical than his first urge and contrary to all rules of flying over hostile territory. He should be flying either high or low and fast. But the urge was so strong that he went down to treetop level, and somehow knew that he was looking for something. There it was! He suddenly spotted the remains of a helicopter scattered over the jungle.

He had no idea how long it had been there, but he felt compelled to check it out. The jungle was so dense that it was impossible to land. While he hovered over the treetops, a member of his crew lowered himself by means of a winch. When the crewman reached the ground he found the wounded men. One by one he secured them to the winch and raised them into the helicopter.

When the last man had been lifted to safety, he secured himself and was pulled up. Just as he left the ground, the VC arrived and started firing at him. The pilot saw what was happening, and as soon as the man was clear of the trees he moved the chopper up and out.

In a few minutes the wounded men were safe in the hospital.

When the Major had finished his story he grasped my hand and said: "Chaplain, I just wanted you to come and help me thank God for His goodness to me. I'm going to serve Him the rest of my life!"

7

Rejoice!

I returned from Vietnam in 1967 and was sent to Fort Benning, Georgia. Twenty-three years earlier I had left there, a handcuffed prisoner. Now I returned as chaplain! It was hard to even remember how I had felt then.

I was assigned as Brigade Chaplain for the twenty-one Officer Candidate companies and the twenty-one non-commissioned Officer Candidate companies. What an opportunity to lead future military leaders to Christ!

It was an exciting challenge, yet I was ever aware of my own shortcomings. I had come to see God's power and presence in and around me, but I was often a reluctant vessel.

I experienced days of discouragement and knew that this was not God's will and plan for me.

I searched the Scriptures for clues. In John 17 I found Jesus praying to the Father for us, His followers. He prayed: ". . .that they might have my joy fulfilled in themselves." That's what I wanted. The joy of the Lord, not just when things were going good, but always. Jesus prayed that I might have it, then what was keeping me from experiencing it continuously?

In Matthew 25:21 I read: ". . .thou hast been faithful over a few things, I will make thee ruler over many things: enter thou into the joy of thy Lord."

So it was a matter of my entering in. I had to do it; it wasn't given me just automatically. "But how do I enter in, Lord?"

In Luke 6:23 Jesus tells us that we are to leap for joy. He even describes when we are to leap for joy: "When you are hungry. . .when men shall hate you. . .when men shall reproach you. . .when they cast out your name as evil. . .rejoice in that day, and leap for joy." I hadn't noticed that in the Bible before.

"How do you expect me to leap for joy under those circumstances, Lord?" It didn't make much sense, but the more I read my Bible, the more Scriptures I found saying the same thing. Was there a principle involved?

I read Paul's second letter to the Corinthians. In chapter 12:9-10 he says: "Most gladly therefore will I rather glory in my infirmities, that the power of Christ may rest upon me. Therefore I take pleasure in infirmities, in reproaches, in necessities, in persecutions, in distresses for Christ's sake: for when I am weak, then am I strong."

Infirmities were the very things that up till now I had not been enjoying. I didn't like it when people turned against me; I didn't like it when accidents happened and things went wrong.

But over and over again I found the words in my Bible: "Rejoice! Thank God for everything." The Psalmist continually spoke of joy in the midst of troubles. "Thou hast turned for me my mourning into dancing," says David in Psalm 30.

69

I was willing to try, but how?

One evening in a small prayer group, I began to laugh. I laughed for fifteen minutes, and while I was laughing I felt God speaking: "Are you glad that Jesus died for your sins?"

"Yes, Lord, I'm glad, I'm glad."

"Does it make you feel good to think of His dying for your sins?"

"Yes, Lord, it really does!"

"Does it make you feel happy to know that He has given you eternal life by His death for you?"

"Yes, Lord, it does!"

"Do you have to strain or try hard to really be filled with joy that He died for you?"

"No, Lord, I'm filled with joy."

I knew that God wanted me to understand how easy it was to be glad that Christ died for me. I could clap my hands, laugh, and sing with thanksgiving for what He had done for me. Nothing in my life was more important; nothing could give me more joy.

I continued laughing, but everything inside me had become very silent. I felt as if God was about to teach me something I'd never known before.

God said: "It really makes you glad that they took My Son and drove nails into His hands. It really makes you glad, doesn't it? It makes you glad that they took My Son and drove nails through His feet. It really makes you glad that they drove a spear through His side and the blood flowed down His body and dripped on the ground. It makes you very happy and you laugh with great joy because they did this to My Son, doesn't it?"

Everything became very silent. I didn't know how to answer.

"It makes you glad that all that was done to My Son, doesn't it?"

Finally I had to say: "Yes, Lord, it does. I don't understand it, Father, but I am glad."

For a moment I wondered if perhaps I had given the wrong answer. Perhaps I had misunderstood.

Then to my great relief I heard Him say: "Yes, my son, I want you to be glad! I want you to be glad!"

I laughed on, and the joy within me increased as I realized that God wanted me to be glad. Then everything became very quiet again, and I knew I was about to learn something.

"Now listen, my son. For the rest of your life when anything happens to you that is any less difficult than what they did to My Son, I want you to be just as glad as you were when I first asked you if you were glad Christ died for you."

I said: "Yes, Lord, I understand. For the rest of my life I am going to be thankful. I'll praise You, I'll rejoice, I'll sing, I'll laugh, I'll shout, I'll be filled with joy for whatever You permit to come into my life."

It was easy to promise to rejoice right then; I was having a wonderful time in prayer. Joy was just flowing over me and through me like a stream.

The next morning I was sitting on the edge of my bed when I heard a voice: "What are you doing?"

"I'm sitting here wishing I didn't have to get up!"

"I thought we made an agreement last night."

"But Lord, I didn't know You meant things like this!"

"Remember what I said, 'in everything.'"

I said: "But Lord, I've got to be honest with You. I've been sitting on the edge of my bed every morning for twenty years wishing I didn't have to get up. I've been thinking how wonderful it would be if I could just lie down for five more minutes."

But the Spirit said: "You are supposed to be thankful that it is time to get up."

"Lord, that's a little beyond my ability to comprehend!"

The Lord is always very patient and kind: "Are you willing to be made willing?"

"Yes, Lord, I really am."

That night I went to bed praying: "Lord, this is a rough one. You're going to have to do it for me. I'll get up anytime You tell me to, but I don't know how to be thankful that it is time to get up."

All I could hear was: "Are you willing?"

"Yes, Lord, I am."

The next morning I woke up and the first thing that popped into my mind was my right big toe. I heard: "See if you can move it." I could.

"Are you thankful that you can move it?"

"Yes, Lord."

"Now try your ankle. Are you thankful?"

"Yes, Lord."

"Now your knee. Are you thankful?"

"Yes, Lord."

"Now see if you can sit up."

"Yes, Lord, I can. But I've got to be honest with You; I still wish I could lie down and go back to sleep."

Very patiently He said: "See if you can stand up. Are you thankful? Now see if you can walk to the bathroom. Look into the mirror. Are you thankful you can see?"

"Hallelujah!"

"Are you glad you can speak and hear?"

"Yes, Lord."

Then everything became very silent. I knew again that out of the silence I was to learn something from God.

"My son, because I love you I am going to teach you to be thankful for everything. You can learn standing right there with all the things you are thankful for, or I can let you go back to bed and not let you move, see, or hear until you learn."

I jumped two feet into the air and said: "Lord, I understand! I am thankful! I will always be thankful."

The next morning, and the next, and the next, the first thing I thought when I woke up was, "Lord, I'm thankful." Never again have I been sorry it is time to get up.

Paul said, "Most gladly therefore will I rather glory in my infirmities." Getting up in the morning had been an infirmity for me. God told me to take it and reverse it from pain into joy, and when I did, the power of Christ and His joy came upon me.

I couldn't wait to share my discovery with others, but the Spirit said no; first I had to learn for myself beyond any doubt how to turn every difficult situation into joy.

I memorized and said over and over to myself the verse from I Thessalonians 5:16-18. "Rejoice evermore. Pray without ceasing. In every thing give thanks: for this is the will of God in Christ Jesus concerning you."

One day as I was nearing a stoplight, it turned amber, but I managed to get through, legally. As I did, a smile of thanksgiving came on my face. I felt the presence of God and He said: "Freeze."

So I froze with that smile on my face.

"Why are you so happy?"

"Lord, I made it through the light, thank You."

"What would you have done if the light had turned sooner, and you had to stop?"

"Lord, I probably would have grumbled a little and wished it had waited for me to get through."

"Don't you know that I control the stoplights? That I control the universe and time itself? The next time a light turns red you must be thankful. You will know it was I who made it turn red."

The next time the light turned red I pulled up and asked God what He wanted me to do with the time.

"See that man walking across the street? He desperately needs your prayers. Just sit there and pray for him."

We say we believe in God. But do we really believe that He controls every detail of our lives, or do we think He's off on more important business? Jesus said that God knows how many hairs we have on our heads. So why can't we believe that He is more intimately concerned with every detail of our lives than we are ourselves? I certainly don't know how many hairs there are on my head!

God is controlling everything and working out everything that happens for good for those who love Him (Romans 8:28).

I was beginning to trust God more, but what about Satan? Can't he sneak in and attack us against God's will?

God permitted Satan to enter into Judas to betray His Son. God permitted Satan to make Peter so weak that he denied having known Jesus. He permitted Satan to enter the hearts of the men who plotted and schemed and crucified Jesus Christ. At any moment God could have stopped them. He could have sent ten thousand angels to sweep aside every plan of Satan. But God didn't stop it. Because He knew that when all the sin and suffering passed through Jesus, it would come out as pure joy, praise, and victory.

Satan can't do a thing to us unless he first gets God's permission. Remember God allowed Satan to test Job. The only time God gives Satan permission is when God sees the tremendous potential in the thing passing through us and coming out as joy, pure joy!

When we begin to realize this, God can bless our lives. The power of the resurrected Christ is in us. Miracles, power, and victory will all be a part of what God does in our lives when we learn to rejoice in all things.

One morning I got into my car to go to work. It wouldn't start. In the Army there is no excuse for being late to work. I said: "Okay, Lord, here I am. You must want me to learn something, so I thank You that this car won't start."

After a while someone came along and helped me get it started.

The next morning the same thing happened. "Thank You, Lord, I know You have some wonderful reason for having me sit here, so I'm going to be filled with joy, and praise You." Again I was able to get it started.

Later that day I took the car to the post garage. I told the manager my problem. He said: "I'm sorry, Chaplain, but the man who works on that kind of car has had a heart attack and is in the hospital. I hate to tell you this, but you'll have to take it to a civilian place." He had a pained expression on his face as he said it. "Chaplain, they know our mechanic is sick, and they'll really sock it to you. They've been doing that to everyone I've sent there."

As I drove toward the "civilian" garage, a voice tried to whisper to me: "Isn't it terrible that those civilians would take advantage of us Army people?"

I told that thought to go back to where it came from, and continued thanking the Lord that He had worked out this whole incident for my personal benefit. I said: "Lord, I know You are in this and I praise You for it."

I pulled in to the garage, and the manager came over with a writing pad in his hand. With a glint in his eye, he said, "Can I help you, Sir?"

I explained my problem to him, and he went through a list of things that "might be wrong."

"We can't repair that part here, so we'll have to send it to another shop. This, however, may not be the problem so we may have to do something else. It could be several different things, but we'll keep looking till we find the trouble."

"How long will it take?"

With a smile he said, "I'm sorry, Sir, but I have no idea. It just depends."

I could imagine the cash register pounding away.

"How much will it cost?"

"I'm sorry, Sir, I have no idea what it may cost."

Our post garage was right. They were ready to get everything out of me that they could. "Thank you, Lord; You had a good reason for this."

I agreed to bring the car back the next morning to leave it there until they could find and fix whatever might be wrong.

I then managed with much difficulty to get the car started. I put it in gear and began to move forward. Just then the manager quickly stepped up and grasped my arm. "Wait a minute! I've just thought of what may be your trouble. Turn off the engine!"

With that he opened the hood and began to poke around with a screwdriver. In a few minutes he said: "Now try it and see how it works."

I stepped on the starter and the engine purred away like it was new.

"Wonderful! How much do I owe you?"

"Not a thing, Sir, glad to do it."

Then the Lord again spoke to my heart: "My son, what I wanted you to know was that you never again have to worry whether anyone will overcharge you, hurt you, or mistreat you unless it is My will. Your life is in the palm of My hand and you can trust Me for all things. As you continue to thank Me in all circumstances you will see how perfectly I work out every detail of your life."

"Hallelujah, Lord!" I bounced up and down on the seat for sheer joy. "Thank You, Lord! Thank You for showing me all these wonderful things."

I rejoiced, and realized that if I had grumbled and complained the entire incident would have profited me absolutely nothing. How many opportunities I had passed up to let God teach me how much He loves me! Most of us go around carrying these opportunities as heavy burdens, but God has ordained through Christ that all of these things can be revolutionized as they pass through us and come out as joy!

How glorious to know that at this very moment God wants to fill our hearts with overflowing joy. Not because of our goodness or our righteousness or our sacrifice. It depends on only one thing, on believing the Lord Jesus. On believing that if the chair collapses under me it is

His will. If the coffee is too hot or the toast soggy, it is His will.

When we begin to really believe that, the power of God begins to break loose in our lives. That's what Jesus tried to explain to us when He said, "Leap for joy when they persecute you. When you are poor. When you have sorrow."

For many years I had suffered with painful headaches. I seldom complained about it; I just thanked God that I wasn't as bad off as some people. One day He said: "Why don't you try praising Me *for* the headache?"

"*For* it?"

"Yes, *for* it."

I began to lift up my thoughts in thanksgiving that God was giving me this headache as an opportunity to increase the power of Christ in my life. The headache got worse. I continued to thank God, but with every thought of praise came increased pain. I realized that Satan and the Spirit of Christ were at war. The pain reached an overwhelming state; I held on to thoughts of praise and thanks. Suddenly I was being flooded with joy. Joy seemed to pour over every cell of my body. I had never experienced such power in joy! I was certain that if I took a step I would rise clear up into the air. And the headache was completely gone!

For fifteen years I had suffered with hay fever at least six months out of the year. Many weeks were so bad that I sneezed and coughed and held a handkerchief to my nose all day long. I had taken shots, tried medicine after medicine, prayed, fasted, and prayed some more. I went to everyone I knew or heard of that would pray for me. Nothing helped.

Why did God let me suffer? Didn't He care that I felt so miserable?

My friend, Chaplain Curry Vaughn, had told me I should believe with him that God would heal me. I avoided seeing Curry when I had one of my attacks because he always kept telling me to go on believing. I had tried believing for fifteen years and didn't know what more I could do.

One day I was scheduled to speak to a noon meeting of men in a local Methodist church. As I drove into Columbus, the water started pouring out of my nose and I sneezed so hard that it was difficult to keep on driving. The thought came: "Praise Me!"

I began to think of how good God was to let me have this infirmity of the flesh. He was permitting me to have it to teach me something. It wasn't an accident of nature that I was allergic to so many things. God had planned it this way for His glory and for my good. "Thank you, Lord, for Your goodness. If You want me to have this I'll just trust You to heal me whenever You want to."

"What do you want me to do?"

"Heal me, Lord."

"Heal you or take away the symptoms?"

"Aren't they the same, Lord?"

"No, they are not."

"Okay, Lord, then just heal me and I won't pay any attention to the symptoms." With that I knew that God had showed me something new and wonderful. Every time I had prayed for healing in the past and tried to believe, I had always been defeated when the symptoms persisted. Now I knew that the symptoms meant nothing. Faith in God's promise was all I needed; then Satan could fake all the symptoms he wanted!

When I arrived at the meeting place my nose was still running like a faucet, and I was sneezing uncontrollably.

I said, "Lord, if you want me to make a fool of myself, I'm willing. I'm leaving my handkerchief here in the car and I'm going in to speak for You."

As I walked toward the church I began to feel better. When the meeting was over I suddenly realized that I had no symptoms of hay fever.

Day after day there were no symptoms. Then one evening as I was preparing to go to a prayer group, my nose started running.

I thought: "Lord, I can't go to the prayer group. Those ladies will think I've done something wrong and You've taken away my faith. They'll gather around and urge me to believe so You can heal me. But Lord, I know You've healed me so I thank You for these symptoms."

At the prayer group one of the sisters began to exhort me to believe.

"But God has healed me," I insisted.

"Then why are you sniffing?"

"I don't know, but God knows, and I'm just praising Him."

On the way home I was continuing to thank Him for running my life just as He wanted to. If He wanted Satan to get in a few licks at me He must have good reason. He had permitted His own Son to suffer for me.

"Son?"

"Yes, Lord,"

"You've been faithful. You will never again have even one symptom unless you need it for your good."

Once again I bounced up and down on the seat. Never again would I pray for healing for the same thing twice. God says, "Ask, and you will receive, that your joy may be full" (John 16:24).

8

Praise Him!

Discovering the power in praise was one of the most exciting experiences I'd ever had; yet every time I wanted to share it with someone, it was as if God was saying: "Hold it. This isn't the time."

When Ron came to see me about his problem he was the picture of misery and despair. "Chaplain, you've got to help me. When I was drafted my wife tried to commit suicide. Now I've received orders for Vietnam, and she says that if I go she'll kill herself. What can I do?"

Ron was an attorney and a member of the bar association. But he had been drafted and preferred to join the Army as a Private. Now he was obviously distraught and unable to handle the situation with his wife.

"Ron, have your wife come in to see me, and I'll see what I can do."

Sue was also a picture of misery. Her body was frail and she sat on the edge of a chair, trembling from head to foot. Tears flowed uncontrollably down her face.

"Chaplain." Her voice was barely audible. "I'm scared; I can't live without Ron."

I looked at her and a wave of compassion brought tears to my eyes. I knew Sue's story. She'd been adopted as a baby, was estranged from her adopted family, and had no one in the world except Ron. The two of them were very much in love and I knew that if Ron went to Vietnam, Sue would stay alone in a rented room in a strange town.

I prayed silently for wisdom to comfort her.

"Tell her to be thankful." I shook my head in disbelief. I must have heard wrong.

"Her, Lord?"

"Yes, you may begin to share with her!" I looked at Sue's tearful face and my heart sank.

"Okay, Lord, I'll trust You."

"Sue, I'm glad you came," I said, smiling with a confidence I didn't feel. "You don't have anything to worry about. Everything is going to be all right."

Sue straightened herself, wiped away her tears, and managed a trembling little smile.

I continued: "What I want you to do is to kneel here with me and thank God that Ron is going to Vietnam."

She looked at me in blank disbelief. I nodded. "Yes, Sue, I want you to thank God."

She immediately began to weep almost hysterically. I calmed her as best I could and began reading to her from the Bible the verses I had learned to trust in over the past few months.

". . .In everything give thanks, for this is the will of God in Christ Jesus concerning you. . .All things work together for good to them that love the Lord." Carefully I tried to show her the wonderful truths I had found to be real.

Nothing seemed to help. Sue believed in God and in Christ, but in her despair her belief was of no comfort. Finally she left my office crying, with no peace of mind and certainly no joy.

"Lord, have I completely misunderstood You? That girl wasn't helped a bit."

"Patience, son. I'm working."

The next day Ron came to my office. "Chaplain, what did you tell Sue? She is worse than she was before."

"I told Sue the solution to her problem and now I'll tell you. I want you to kneel down and thank God that you're going to Vietnam and that Sue is so upset that she is threatening to kill herself."

Ron didn't see my point either. Carefully we went over the Scriptures: ". . .This is the will of God concerning you."

Ron said: "Now I understand why Sue didn't understand. I don't understand either." And he left.

Two days later they came back. "Sir, we are desperate. You must do something to help us."

They were both hoping that I as chaplain would be able to put in a plea for another assignment for Ron.

Again I explained to them the only solution God was letting me hold up before them. "All things work together for good to them that love the Lord."

"If you can only believe that God is really working this thing out for the best for both of you, then all you have to do is trust Him and begin to thank Him - regardless of what the situation looks like".

Ron and Sue looked at each other. "What do we have to lose, Honey?" Ron said. We knelt and Sue prayed:

"Lord, I thank you that Ron is going to Vietnam. It must be Your will. I sure don't understand, but I'll try."

Then Ron prayed: "Lord, this is very strange to me, too, but I trust You. Thank You that I am going to Vietnam and that Sue is so upset. Thank You that she might even try to hurt herself."

I had a feeling Ron and Sue were not as convinced as I was, but I thanked the Lord that they were trying.

They left my office, and later I heard what had happened.

Ron and Sue had gone into the chapel and knelt together at the altar. There they had turned their lives and each other over to God in a deeper commitment than ever before and now Sue had the strength to pray: "God, I thank You that Ron is going to Vietnam. You know how much I will miss him. You know I don't have a father or mother or brother or sister or family of any kind. I will trust You, Lord."

Ron prayed: "God, I do thank You. I give Sue over to You. She is Yours and I'll trust You to take care of her."

With that they rose from the altar. Ron went through the chapel and headed for his unit while Sue came back to the waiting room next to my office. She needed to sit quietly and collect her thoughts. While she sat there a young soldier came in and asked for the chaplain. Sue told him that I was busy. "But if you wait a little while, I'll tell him you're here," she offered.

"I'll wait," said the young soldier. He looked distressed and Sue asked: "What is your problem?"

"My wife wants a divorce."

Sue shook her head: "It won't do much good to see *that* Chaplain," she said, but the soldier wasn't easily discouraged, and while they were waiting he took out his billfold and began to show Sue pictures of his wife and children. When he turned to the next picture Sue screamed: "Who is that?"

"That's my mother".

"That is *m*y mother", said Sue, shaking with emotion.

"That couldn't be," the soldier replied. "I don't have a sister."

"It is; I know it is!"

"What makes you think that?"

When I was a little girl I happened to find a piece of paper in my parents' desk that showed I was adopted. In the upper right-hand corner was a picture of my real mother. That's her. It's the same lady."

And it was.

Further checking revealed that Sue had been promised for adoption before she was born and her natural mother had never seen her. She had no idea where Sue was and had never heard anything about her since the day she was born.

Now Sue had a brother, a real brother, and with him came a whole family.

Was it coincidence? There are more than two hundred million people in the United States. What would be the odds against that particular soldier walking in the door to my office just as Sue had made a covenant with God to praise Him for her loneliness and lack of family?

But that wasn't all. As Ron walked back into his unit, he ran into an old friend from law school who was now a legal officer.

"Hi, old buddy, where are you going?" he said as he met Ron.

"Praise God, I'm going to Vietnam," Ron answered. They talked some more, and the friend persuaded Ron to ask for a transfer so that he could work with him in the legal office.

Ron and Sue did not have to be separated. And no longer did Sue have to cling to Ron in fear of losing Him. She had come to have a joyous confidence in Jesus Christ and went about everywhere praising Him.

Later an Officer Candidate came to my office. He openly wept for a long time. "Sir, you must help me. My wife has been asking for a divorce. Her lawyer has just sent me the papers to sign. I just can't keep on with the Officer Candidate program. I don't even want to stay in the Army. Please help me."

"I know just how to get your problem solved. Let's kneel down and thank God that your wife wants a divorce."

He didn't understand any better than Sue and Ron did. Carefully we went over the Scriptures together. At last he decided he might as well try it. We knelt together and he prayed, turning the whole situation over to God and thanking Him for having allowed it to happen.

When he returned to his unit he was so shaken emotionally that they gave him the rest of the day off. He went to his bed and lay there, repeating over and over, "Thank you, Lord, that my wife wants a divorce. I surely don't understand it, but Your Word says I should thank You for all things, so I'll do it." All day long he thought the same things over and over. That night he couldn't sleep, so he went on thanking God. The next day he went through training in a daze. "Lord, You know I don't understand, but I thank You anyhow."

That evening he was sitting in the mess hall having dinner. As he was eating, it suddenly hit him. "Lord, you really *must* know what is better for me, much more than I do. I *know* all of this must be your will. *Thank* You, Lord; now I understand!"

At that moment another candidate tapped him on the shoulder and told him to come to the telephone.

In all the weeks he'd been a candidate, no one had ever wanted him on the phone.

When he lifted the receiver there was someone weeping on the other end. "Honey, can you ever forgive me? I don't want a divorce!"

A lady came reluctantly to see me. One of her friends had almost dragged her into my office. She told me that she had seriously been considering suicide, but didn't see what good it would do to talk about it.

Little by little she gave me the details. Her husband had fathered an illegitimate child by another woman. The child was being kept by her husband's parents. Every time she went to visit her in-laws, there was the child. To make things worse, the child's mother usually showed up at the same time. Even though they were having financial difficulties, her husband was sending money to his parents to help take care of his illegitimate child. She couldn't live with this constant pain inside anymore.

"Don't worry," I said to her. "You won't have to; there is a solution to your problem."

She looked up, rather surprised. "What is it?"

"Let us kneel here and thank God that your husband fathered this child." Again I went over the Scriptures on thanking God for all things. Wiping away her tears, she finally agreed to try it. We prayed, and she left the office determined to let God work out the problems in her life.

The next morning I called to see how she was doing.

"Wonderful!"

"You are?"

"Yes, Sir, I got up this morning just filled with joy!"

"What happened?"

"When I got home yesterday I began to think what I could do now that I am thankful for my husband's baby. I decided that if I was really thankful, I ought to do something about it. So I sat down and wrote a check to my in-laws and told them to use it for the baby. This morning I feel absolutely glorious."

The next day I called her again, and she said: "I feel even better than yesterday."

"What have you done now?"

"I started thinking of a lady who lives near me who has a retarded child. I went to see her this morning and asked if I could help with the child. She was so amazed she didn't know what to say. I stayed and started to do what I could."

"Do you know what to do for a retarded child?"

"Yes, Sir. I have a master's degree in working with special children."

"Have you worked with children since you graduated?"

"No, Sir. This is the first child I've ever worked with."

"Now do you understand why God permitted that thing to happen in your life?"

"Yes, Sir, I do, and now I really praise Him!"

From that day on she was a changed woman. Those who knew her before said she had always looked and acted as if she was in great pain. Now they say she looks and acts as though she has discovered some wonderful secret, and people are being drawn to Christ through her radiance and joy.

Jesus didn't promise to change the circumstances around us, but He did promise great peace and pure joy to those who would learn to believe that God actually controls all things.

The very act of praise releases the power of God into a set of circumstances and enables God to change them if this is His design. Very often it is our attitudes that hinder the solution of a problem. God is sovereign and could certainly cut across our wrong thought patterns and attitudes. But His perfect plan is to bring each of us into fellowship and communion with Him, and so He allows circumstances and incidents which will bring our wrong attitudes to our attention.

I have come to believe that the prayer of praise is the highest form of communion with God, and one that always releases a great deal of power into our lives. Praising Him is not something we do because we feel good; rather it is an act of obedience. Often the prayer of praise is done in sheer teeth-gritting willpower; yet when we persist in it, somehow the power of God is released into us and into the situation. At first in a trickle perhaps, but later in a growing stream that finally floods us and washes away the old hurts and scars.

One Army wife came to me, convinced that her problem had but one solution.

Her husband had developed an excessive drinking problem and for the past several years had been an alcoholic. Often he would pass out drunk on the living room floor where the wife or his teen-age children would find him, stark naked. In this condition he'd also been found in the hallway of the apartment house where several other families lived.

In final desperation the wife decided to take the children and leave. Friends persuaded her to at least come talk to me first.

"Whatever you say, Chaplain, don't tell me to stay with him," she said. "I just can't do it."

"I don't really care whether you stay with him or not," I said. "I just want you to thank God that your husband is like he is." Carefully I explained what the Bible had to say about thanking God for all things and that if she tried it, God would be able to solve her problem in the best way.

She thought it sounded ridiculous, but finally agreed to kneel while I prayed that God would release in her enough faith to believe that He is a God of love and power who holds the universe in His hand.

At last she said, "I do believe."

Two weeks later I called her.

"I feel absolutely marvelous," she said. "My husband is a different man. He hasn't had a drink in two weeks."

"That's wonderful," I said. "I'd like to talk to him."

"What do you mean?" She sounded surprised.

"I just think it would be good if I talked to your husband about the power that is working in your lives."

"Didn't you tell him already?" She sounded puzzled.

"No, I haven't met him yet."

"Chaplain, this is a miracle," she cried out. "The day I was in your office he came home from work and for the first time in seven years he didn't go to the refrigerator for a beer. Instead he went into the living room and talked to the children. I was sure you had talked to him."

Our prayer of praise had released God's power to work in another person's life. The wife was openly crying over the telephone.

"Praise God, Chaplain," she sobbed, "Now I know God works out every detail of our lives."

A young soldier collapsed with a serious heart problem and was taken to the Fort Benning Hospital. He was released, but had to come back for frequent checkups and eventually was scheduled to go to another hospital for heart surgery. The news filled him with despair, and he began drinking. His despair increased until he decided to leave. He stole clothes from some of the men in the barracks and took off in the First Sergeant's car, which he wrecked totally.

The unhappy soldier was caught and put in the stockade to await trial. There another soldier led him to Christ. I went to see him, and he was still feeling depressed and afraid that he had messed up his life so thoroughly that he couldn't be of any use to anyone.

"Your sins are forgiven and forgotten," I said. "Don't think of your past as a chain around your neck. Thank God for every detail of your life and believe He has permitted all of these things in order to bring you to the place where you are now."

Together we searched the Scriptures for God's word on all things working out for those who love Him.

"And that doesn't just mean things that happen after you've asked God to take over your life," I said. "God is able to use even our past

94

mistakes and failures when we release them to Him with *thanksgiving*."

He understood, and began to thank God in earnest for everything that had happened. As his trial neared, his defense attorney told him the best he could hope for was a five-year sentence and dishonorable discharge. The soldier remained undaunted and insisted that whatever happened, God had full control of his life and would work out whatever would be for his good.

The General Court-martial had a surprise ending. General Court-martial is never held unless the military authorities believe that the crime warrants severe punishment. This soldier was sentenced to six months in the local stockade and no discharge from the Army.

With Chaplain Curry Vaughan I went to visit him in the stockade. We thought we were there to encourage him; instead he encouraged us. He was filled with joy and it was catching. Soon the stockade rang with our laughter. The young soldier couldn't stand still; he laughed and ran and skipped around the visiting room.

Before we got ready to leave we asked how he was feeling. He had been scheduled for heart surgery and medically speaking was still in need of attention. He confessed that he felt very weak physically, and often his heart was troubling him. But he said: "It is wonderful. God is taking care of me."

We asked if he would like prayer for healing and he said:

"Please do; I believe God will heal me."

We placed our hands on him and believed that God, through Christ, was right there healing him. The soldier smiled radiantly and said: "I believe it is done."

A few weeks later I talked to the man's Company Commander.

"I believe it's a waste of government money to keep this man in the stockade."

"Why, Chaplain?" he said.

"He isn't the same man who stole clothes and a car and wrecked it. He's completely changed."

The Commander agreed and had the man released. A week later I asked him how he felt.

"Chaplain, I used to get tired after walking one hundred yards. Now I can run and I never seem to get tired. God has healed me."

Wherever I went I now shared what I had discovered about the power of praise. I was beginning to learn that praise was not just a form of worship or prayer, but also a way of waging spiritual warfare. Often when someone began to praise God for the problems that faced him, he found that Satan increased his attacks and the situation appeared to become worse instead of better. Many who tried the way of praise became discouraged and were unable to hold on to their belief that God was in charge.

Others simply didn't understand and refused to try praising God for unpleasant things. "It just doesn't make sense," they'd say. "I'm not going to praise God for something I just don't believe He has anything to do with. How can God have anything to do with my broken arm or my wrecked car or my husband's horrible temper? I'd be foolish to thank Him for something like that."

Of course it doesn't make sense. The question is, does it work? It didn't make much sense when Jesus said, "Leap for joy when you are hungry or poor or persecuted." Yet He very definitely told us to do just that. In Nehemiah 8:10 I read: "The joy of the Lord is your strength."

The enemy's arrows just can't penetrate the joy of someone who is praising the Lord. In II Chronicles 20 we read how a whole army was defeated when the Israelites simply praised the Lord and believed Him when He said that the battle wasn't theirs, but His.

The message is just as clear today. The battle isn't ours; it is God's. While we praise Him, He sends our enemies scurrying.

It was discouraging and sad to see those who refused to praise the Lord. My heart ached for them in their hopeless situations of suffering and misery. I asked God to give me wisdom to understand why they couldn't accept the way of praise, and also asked Him to teach me better ways of leading others to praising Him.

Nearly seven months after I first had the experience of laughing with joy in the Spirit, I went to a Camp Farthest Out Retreat. I was looking forward to a time of resting and rejoicing in the fellowship of brothers and sisters in Christ.

While I sat in the back of the auditorium during a healing service, I closed my eyes and on the screen of my inner vision God painted a picture.

I saw a beautiful, bright summer day. The air was filled with light, and I had a sense of everything being very beautiful. Up above was a heavy, solid black cloud beyond which nothing could be seen. A ladder extended from the ground up into the black cloud. At the base of the ladder were hundreds of people trying to get a chance at climbing the ladder. They had heard that above the blackness there was something more beautiful than anything a human eye had ever seen, something that brought unbelievable joy to those who reached it. As person after person tried to ascend they quickly climbed to the lower edge of the clouds. The crowd watched to see what would happen.

In a short while the person would come wildly sliding down the ladder and fall into the crowd scattering people in all directions. They reported that once they got into the blackness they lost all sense of direction.

My time finally came, and as I made my way up the ladder into the blackness it grew so intense that I could feel its power nearly forcing me to give up and slide back. But step by step I continued upward until suddenly my eyes beheld the most intense brightness I had ever seen. It was a brilliant whiteness too glorious to describe in words. As I came out above the dark cloud I realized that I could walk on top of it. As I looked into the brightness I was able to walk without difficulty. When I looked down to examine the nature of the cloud I immediately began to sink. Only by looking at the brightness could I stay on top.

Then the scene changed and I was back looking at all three levels from a distance.

"What does it all mean?" I asked, and the answer came:

"The brightest sunshine below the cloud is the light that many Christians live in and accept as normal. The ladder is the ladder of praising Me. Many try to climb and learn to praise Me in all things. At first they are very eager, but when they get into things that they don't understand they become confused and cannot hold on. They lose faith and go sliding back. As they fall, they injure other people who have been hoping to find a way to live in continual joy and praise.

"Those who make it through those difficult times reach a new world and realize that the life they once thought of as normal cannot be compared to the life I have prepared for those who praise Me and believe that I carefully watch over them. He who reaches the light of the heavenly kingdom can walk on top of difficulties no matter how dark they may seem as long as he keeps his eyes off the problem and on My victory in Christ. No matter how difficult it may seem to trust Me to work in every detail of your life, keep clinging to the ladder of praise and move upwards!"

I was half-dazed by the vision and the explanation and wondered how soon God would let me share it with someone.

At the camp I met a woman who was faced with problems of illness and family difficulties at home. She found it hard to believe that praising God was going to do any good.

Inwardly I asked for guidance, and God said, "Tell her!"

So I told her. "You'll be the first one to hear this," I said, and as she listened I could see how the heaviness literally left and her face and eyes lit up with a look of joyous expectancy.

In Ephesians, chapters one and two, I found my vision described in slightly different words by Paul:

". . .Blessed (Praised!) be the God and Father of our Lord Jesus Christ, who hath blessed us with all spiritual blessings in heavenly places in Christ: . . .he hath chosen us in him before the foundation of the world, that we should be holy and without blame. . .To the praise of the glory of his grace. . .that in. . .the fulness of times he might gather together in one all things in Christ. . .That we should be to the praise of his glory, who first trusted in Christ. . .that you may know. . .what is the exceeding greatness of his power to us-ward who believe, according to the working of his mighty power, which he wrought in Christ, when he raised him from the dead and set him at his own right hand in the heavenly places, Far above all principality and power, and might, and dominion. . .And hath raised us up together, and made us sit together in heavenly places in Christ Jesus." Jesus Christ is raised above all the powers of darkness, and according to God's word, our rightful inheritance is right there above the darkness together in Christ. The ladder is praise!

I was becoming more aware of the power of praise, but also aware of some of the enemy's snares.

At the time I began to search my Bible for insight into praise I was also led to Scriptures describing the power we have received in Christ over the forces of darkness. I had long been aware of the passage in Mark 16 where Jesus speaks of the signs that will follow those who believe in Him: "In my name shall they cast out devils; they shall speak with new tongues; they shall take up serpents; and if they drink any deadly thing, it shall not hurt them; they shall lay hands on the sick, and they shall recover."

I had prayed asking God to show me if this was all valid for me in the twentieth century, and if it was, when and how to use it.

I found that I often became uneasy when I was around certain people, and asking God, I got the strong impression that what was wrong with them was of a demonic nature.

I prayed that if I ever came face-to-face with someone like that during a prayer-session that God would tell me what to do.

An Army wife was deserted by her husband who left her with three children. In desperation she tried to kill herself. She was rushed to the hospital and her life was saved. Friends brought her to see me after she got home. She was the picture of despair. Her friends had told me that for several years they had never seen her smile. I began speaking to her about the way of praising God but soon felt compelled to stop. I looked into her eyes and suddenly sensed that there was something very wrong and very evil within her.

Within me was a sense of fear; I realized that I was actually face-to-face with evil.

"Lord," I prayed within. "I've come this far, I can't go back now, so I'll step out in faith trusting that You'll do the work."

Looking straight into the woman's eyes I spoke out loud commanding the vicious spirit to get out of her in the name of the Lord Jesus Christ and by the power of His shed blood.

Her glassy eyes suddenly cleared, and she could listen as I explained that God could work all things for good if she would only trust and praise Him.

She now was free to understand, and smiled with a beautiful radiance. Jesus Christ had broken the bondage of darkness that had threatened her life.

Chaplain Curry Vaughan, Jr., had begun to experience the power of praise in his own life. Soon after he had started praising God for his difficulties, he arrived home one evening to learn that his two-year-old daughter had swallowed a glassful of mineral spirits, a type of high-grade turpentine. She had already been rushed to the hospital. Curry jumped into his car and raced full speed to be with her. His mind was swirling with thoughts of fear and worry. He suddenly realized what he was doing, slowed the car to normal speed, and praised the Lord for what had happened.

At the hospital they pumped out his daughter's stomach, x-rayed her and told Curry that two things were bound to happen. First, she would run a high fever that night; second, there was a ninety-five percent chance that she would develop pneumonia.

Curry and his wife Nancy took their daughter home, prepared to watch her very closely as the doctors had ordered.

At home Curry took his daughter in his arms and prayed: "Heavenly Father, I know that Satan has tried to attack me once again, and I have praised You! Now I claim in the name of Jesus that Virginia will not get a fever and she will not get pneumonia." The next morning Virginia woke up as bright and chipper as ever. She had suffered no ill effects.

A successful businessman came to see me about his teen-age daughter. I knew the family and knew that their daughter had received more than the average amount of love and care, yet she had developed a violent hatred of her younger sister. She would lash out and strike her with whatever heavy object she could find.

The distraught parents had taken her to the psychiatrist for treatment, kept her on tranquilizers and prayed for years that God would help them find a solution to their terrible problem.

They realized the danger as the violent outbursts increased.

I met with both parents and challenged them to try the one thing they had failed to do.

"What is that?" they both asked.

"Thank the Lord that He has given you this child to meet your need. Really praise Him for knowing exactly what would be the greatest blessing to your family."

At first they thought this was completely beyond what they could do. They had tried for years to solve the problem, and knew of no way to suddenly be glad that everything was exactly the way it was. We went through the Scriptures together and then prayed that God would work a miracle and help them to thank Him.

A miracle did happen. They began to feel and be thankful. They practiced this daily for two weeks. Instead of constant worry and fear they experienced peace and joy.

One evening they were in the living room. Their oldest daughter stood in the middle of the floor holding a potted flower. She looked at them, and when she had their attention she smiled and dropped the pot in the middle of the rug. Dirt, glass and flowers went in all directions. The girl stood smiling, waiting for their reaction. Both parents had given themselves so completely to the practice of praising God that they automatically said, at the same time: "Thank You, Lord."

The daughter looked at them in amazement. Then she lifted her head and, looking toward heaven, she said: "Thank You, Lord, for teaching me." From that very moment she began to get well.

Her parents came to me rejoicing. The power of praise had worked. For years Satan had held the family in bondage through that girl. Now his spell was broken. In James we read that we are to draw near to God and resist Satan. In Romans

12:21 Paul describes how: "Don't allow yourself to be overpowered by evil. Take the offensive - overpower evil with good!"

Some have asked me if this principle of praise isn't just another way to talk about the power of positive thinking. Far from it. Praising God for every circumstance does not mean we close our eyes to the difficulties. In his letter to the Philippians Paul says to worry about nothing, but "In everything by prayer and supplication with *thanksgiving* let your requests be made known to God. And the peace of God, which passes all understanding, will keep your hearts and your minds in Christ Jesus."

Looking only at the good side of every situation is often a dangerous way of trying to escape the reality of it. When we praise God we thank Him *for* our situation, not in spite of it.

We are not trying to avoid our dilemmas. Rather Jesus Christ is showing us a way to overcome them.

There is a ladder of praise and I believe that everyone without exception can begin to praise God right now in whatever situation he may find himself.

For our praise to reach the perfection God wants for us, it needs to be free of any thoughts of reward. Praise is not another way of bargaining with the Lord. We don't say, "Now we've praised You in the middle of this mess, so get us out of it!"

Praising God with a pure heart means we must let God cleanse our hearts from impure motives and hidden designs. We have to experience the dying to self so that we can live again in Christ in newness of mind and spirit.

Dying to self is a progressive journey, and I have come to believe it is traveled only through praise.

God is calling us to praise Him, and the highest form of praise is the one Paul exhorts us to give in Hebrews 13:15: "By (Christ) therefore let us offer the sacrifice of praise to God continually, that is, the fruit of our lips, giving thanks to his name."

The sacrifice of praise is offered when all is darkness around us. It is offered of a heavy heart, unto God because He is God and Father and Lord.

As we begin to praise Him, on whatever step of the ladder we may be, His Holy Spirit begins to fill our beings more and more.

To continually praise Him means a steady decreasing of self and an increase of the presence of Christ within us until with Peter we rejoice with joy unspeakable and full of glory.

If this book has been a blessing to you, please let us know. Each month we prepare *Praise News* in which we share new things that we learn about praise. We will be pleased to send this to you at no charge if you request it. You will also receive information about any new books.

Write to:
Merlin Carothers
PO Box 2518
Escondido, CA 92033-2518
Or visit us at our website at:
www.merlincarothers.com

Additional bestsellers by Merlin Carothers:

PRISON TO PRAISE GIANT PRINT.... $6.95

POWER IN PRAISE $6.95
Three Million National Bestseller. A simple clear explanation of how and why the principles introduced in *Prison to Praise* work in every day life.

POWER IN PRAISE GIANT PRINT...... $7.95

ANSWERS TO PRAISE $6.95
Overjoyed Christians felt compelled to share with Merlin the "signs and wonders" they experienced while practicing the teachings of praise.

PRAISE WORKS $6.95
More letters from an assortment of thousands illustrate the secret of *freedom through praise*!

WALKING AND LEAPING $6.95
When Merlin and his family roll over a hill in their new car and trailer they praised the Lord and miracles happen!

BRINGING HEAVEN INTO HELL $6.95
Merlin shares new discoveries of how the Holy Spirit sheds light from heaven in the midst of a personal hell.

VICTORY ON PRAISE MOUNTAIN $6.95
Spontaneous praise often leads into valleys that are direct paths to higher ground.

MORE POWER TO YOU............................ **$6.95**
Written for persons in every day places who need more power in their every day lives.

WHAT'S ON YOUR MIND? **$6.95**
Would you be ashamed for everyone you know to see your thoughts? If so, you urgently need to read and understand this book.

LET ME ENTERTAIN YOU **$6.95**
After years of serving the Lord, Merlin was eager to retire. He wanted to rest, relax and enjoy a quiet life, but God had other plans for him.

FROM FEAR TO FAITH (Revised).......... **$8.95**
God wants to be intimately involved in your life and help you have victory over your problems?

YOU CAN BE HAPPY NOW..................... **$8.95**
Is happiness evading you? Discover how you can find enduring happiness despite personal hardships.

THE BIBLE ON PRAISE **$3.75**
A beautiful and colorful booklet featuring Merlin's favorite verses on praise from thirty-eight books of the Bible. The envelope that is included makes this an ideal greeting card.

PRAISE CLASSIC **$9.95**
Prison to Praise and *Power in Praise* are combined in a beautiful hardcover edition.

JUST RELEASED!

SECRET SINS $8.95
As you read this book you will be especially pleased to learn that God has provided a simple way for many of us to be delivered from our secret sins. Once you read it, you will agree that everyone you know needs to read this book.

TRACTS AVAILABLE:
Many people have ordered and distributed thousands of these powerful witnessing tracts. They report that as a result of reading these tracts many people have decided to seek Jesus as their Lord and Savior.

HERE ANIMAL (100) $5.00
A prisoner hated everyone so much that he became more like an animal than a human. Then a miracle happened - nothing else could explain the change in him.

AMAZING STORY (100)............................$5.00
Marilyn met the Savior while in a mental hospital, in a remarkable delivery from a "hopeless" ward.

SHOULD I PRAISE GOD? (100)..............$5.00
Why isn't God answering my prayers? Discover why God wants you to trust Him and stop asking "why?"

AWARD WINNING MOVIE

A true story based on the book with more than 15 million copies in print!

A First Place award by "National Religious Broadcasters."

An Angel award by "Excellence in Media."

A First Place Covenant Award by "The Southern Baptist Radio and Television Commission."

ISBN 0-943026-33-4

If you didn't believe in miracles beforc, you will after watching *Prison to Praise*.

A sixty minute video that is loved by children and adults.

Available for $12.95 from:
Foundation of Praise
PO Box 2518 Dept. M-B1
Escondido CA 92033-2518
or your local bookstore.

Please enclose $3.50
for shipping on all orders

The Foundation of Praise is now supplying free copies of this book to:

PRISONS: Federal, State, County and many foreign countries.

HOSPITALS: Civilian and Veterans'.

MILITARY: Bases throughout the United States and the world.

CRISIS PREGNANCY CENTERS: These books are saving lives!

You can help supply free books to those who desperately need help through your contributions to:

Foundation of Praise
P O Box 2518
Escondido, CA 92033-2518

Many thousands of readers have accepted Jesus as their Savior while they read *Prison to Praise*. I pray that you too have received something from the Lord.

Since I wrote *Prison to Praise*, twenty-seven years ago, my conviction has steadily grown stronger that a dynamic force is released in our lives when we praise the Lord for everything.

If you haven't received Jesus as your Savior and Lord, please pray with me:

Dear God, I confess that I am a sinner. Please forgive all my sins - the ones I can remember and the ones I can't remember. Thank You, Jesus, that You lived a sinless life and took the punishment for my sins. I receive You as my Savior and the free gift of eternal life that You give me. I want to live for You, to serve You and to honor You. I receive Your Holy Spirit and I will follow You.

Once we have accepted Christ as our Savior, the Holy Spirit begins to work in our hearts. If you want His work in you to accomplish God's purpose, I **strongly recommend**:

I. Earnestly study God's Word every day. Powerful forces will strive to convince you that you do not need to do so. The Bible says of itself that it is "God's breath." Without that heavenly breath we can soon become lukewarm Christians.

II. Pray regularly - Jesus did. He rose before daylight to talk with God. He asked His disciples why they couldn't pray **at least** one hour. Never let yourself be deceived into thinking that you are too busy or that prayer doesn't work. Pray fervently, and God will reveal Himself to you in new and exciting ways.

III. Turn your back on evil of every kind. Evil has an insidious way of making itself appear to be acceptable, if we fellowship with it. For example, many television programs and movies are designed to make evil look attractive or even good.

IV. Witness for Him daily! God forgave us of our sins and gave us the free gift of eternal life. In return, He asks us to tell others about His Son. Many Christians spend much time in learning how to be a stronger Christian, but never learn that one of our greatest sources of strength is to bring other people to Christ! Don't miss out on this blessing!

I had prayed for God to make me more loving, and had come to think of myself as a not too unloving sort of person. In fact, as I traveled and ministered to thousands of people all of whom seemed to be blessed, I rejoiced that I was able to feel more love for others all the time.

Then one day I was faced with an individual so miserable and repulsive that I cringed at the sight and realized to my horror that I felt no love for this creature, but only wished that she would disappear as soon as possible.

She was a girl who had been brought to my office with her soldier boyfriend. Her face was caked with old makeup and dirt, her hair hung like strands of wire, and her clothes were filthy and torn. Her legs were scarred and smeared with dirt, and the odor from her body filled the room. The expression on her face was sullen and hateful, and her eyes were swollen from crying.

This poor creature had come to Fort Benning to tell the soldier that she was expecting his baby. The boy admitted that he was responsible for her condition, but had flatly refused to marry her. The girl had flown into a rage and threatened to kill him and then herself. She had already had another baby out of wedlock, and this time she was determined to either get married or die.

I looked at her and thought I had never seen anyone so unlovable, so desperate, so frightened, and so lonely. Yet, the very thought of praying for her was offensive to me. I didn't want to touch her.

"Lord," I cried inwardly, "why did you bring her to me?"

"She's one of my children," came the answer. "She is lost and in need of my love and healing. I brought her here for you to love her and tell her of my love."

The painful realization hit me suddenly. I had boasted to myself of being able to love, yet now I cringed at the sight of one who desperately needed to be loved.

"O, Lord," I cried inside, "forgive me, and thank you for showing me just how shallow and selfish my love is. Take my unlovingness and fill me with your love for her."

The girl was sobbing and her eyes looked dull behind the swollen lids smeared with mascara.

"Please, Sir," she said, "do something!"

"Do you believe in God?"

She nodded and whispered, "Yes, I do."

"Do you believe He can help you?"

She hesitated, then spoke slowly. "I know He could help me, but I don't think He'd want to. I used to be a Christian, but look at me now. Even if He wanted to help me, what could He do to get me out of this mess?"

"God *can* help you, and He *wants* to," I said with an assurance I didn't yet feel.

She shook her head and her shoulders sagged in utter hopelessness.

"Please," I said, "try to understand that God loves you. He will fill you with His joy and peace and meet your every need before you leave my office today."

The girl stared, open-mouthed, and the soldier looked as if he thought I was going to force him to marry the girl.

"God has brought you here today," I continued. "He has permitted all the troubles in your life just so that you could understand how much He loves you. He has a wonderful plan for your life, and if you begin to trust Him and thank Him for everything that has happened to you, you will discover that God is helping you right now."

"Thank Him for this?" Her eyes blazed in sudden anger again. "All I want is for this man to marry me so my child will have a name."

"Look here." I showed her the underlined verse in my open Bible. "In every thing give thanks, for this is the will of God in Christ Jesus concerning you" (I Thess. 5:18). I flipped the pages to Romans 8:28. "All things work together for good to them that love God."

Her eyes stared in blank mistrust, and I suddenly realized how futile it was to speak to this wounded creature about God's love or any kind of love. She didn't know the meaning of the word. Only God could light the spark of understanding in her mind.

"May I pray for you?"

She nodded dully. "Sure, why not?"

I moved to place my hand on her head, and

as I looked down and saw just how dirty and in need of scrubbing she was. The twinge of revulsion made me shudder.

"Oh, Lord," I whispered, "how endless your love is for us ---so much greater than the little love we are capable of on our own. Please, God, let your love touch her now, and teach me to love her."

Then I placed my hand firmly on her head and began to pray...

Read the amazing results of this prayer, in my next book, *Power in Praise*.